The
GOD
for
Every
Day

The GOD for Every Day

by
William Maestri

THE THOMAS MORE PRESS
Chicago, Illinois

ISBN 0-88347-123-X

Table of Contents

For Ferdinand, Elaine, and
Brian
"The Family"

INTRODUCTION

IF there is one predominant feeling or mood that characterizes our present experience, it is powerlessness. Life has become so big and complex that the day-to-day events and activities that consume our time seem to be out of control. They are especially out of our control. From major decisions, such as the Panama Canal and Salt II treaties, to the everyday concerns of food prices, gas, and medical costs, one thing is clear: events happen to us and not because of us. More and more we find ourselves using the indefinite collective pronoun "they". "They" have decided this or that issue. The reason why this came to pass was because "they" willed it so. The use of "they" in referring to decision-makers and the seats of power is ominous indeed. Power has lost its identity and with it its accountability. There is literally no one answerable for the steward-ship of power.

We were led to believe that the twin gospels of science and technology would lead us into the promised land. Science and technology would deliver all the goods we need for meaning and contentment. However, skepticism has grown among the faithful. The crises of energy and ecology, along with the ever present danger of a nuclear holocaust, evoke the Doubting Thomas within. On a day-to-day level, so many of the technological gadgets that clutter our terrain are used but not understood. We use the television, car, air conditioner and stove, but when broken we must call in the expert to restore them to usability. We become increasingly alienated, strangers in our fabricated world. This only increases our sense of powerlessness.

The mood of powerlessness has serious consequences for our spiritual life. An environment of powerlessness leads to despair. Next to lovelessness, despair is the most uncharacteristic of Christian dispositions. Despair is a heart without hope. Hope is the heart of the Christian. Hope is not sentimentality or simple good cheer. Hope is deeper than a Pollyanna belief that tomorrow will be better than today. Hope is tougher and more tenacious. Hope does not set time limits or look for immediate results. Hope, like love, endures all things and is open to the future. Hope does not depend on immediate results, but has faith in things not yet seen. Hope is our faith, in the power of the future from the God who is Absolute Future. Hope is grounded in the here-and-not-yet Kingdom of God. Hope sees the power of this world as weakness and its wisdom as foolishness. The Crucified and Risen

One is the power, wisdom, and hope for human-kind.

The theme that unites this book is as follows: Christianity is a way of life. And the God that we celebrate, who revealed himself in Jesus and abides with us in the power of the Spirit, is at the center of our everyday concerns. From God there is no private moment or secret place. All is known to him through whom we live, move and have our being. Our God is a Father for every-day.

We live in an age which often seeks mean-ing and truth in the loud and spectacular. Therefore, it is quite natural that we should search for God among superstars and supermen. The presence of God is not found amid signs and wonders, but the Kingdom is still among us and within us. God is in our midst in a manger, vulnerable and in need. The human face of God is of humble origin and ordinary circumstances. Ultimately, God is with us and for us as the Aban-doned One of the Cross and the hope of an empty tomb. In other words, it is the ordinary, every-day realities that serve as the horizon for our en-counter with God. The everyday, with its banali-ty, profaneness and ordinariness, is the arena of our existence and the turf of our salvation. The everyday and the ordinary are the least of our brethren through whom we encounter and minister to Jesus. The everyday can be a cause of our powerlessness. The everyday sets limits to our vision and potential. We can be blinded to the possibilities and prompting of the Holy Spirit. The sacredness and power of each person can be lost in the demands of daily routines. We can experience a loss of personal power and growth in which *all* of life becomes mere routine. However, it is *in* the everyday and ordinary that we are sent. Each Eucharistic celebration ends with a commission; a sending forth—"Go in peace to love and serve the Lord and one another." We are sent into the everyday and the familiar with the message of hope. We are empowered to speak and give witness concerning the One who lives in unapproachable light and at the same time dwells within us. In effect, we are to be the agents of redeeming the everyday.

In the following pages there is an absence of technical theologizing. The need for such theological work is essential to the life of the Church. Theology is "faith seeking understanding" about the Ancient One who "is ever old and ever new." However, the need to do theology is not the privilege of the few but the responsibility of all. If theology calls us to talk about God in a reflective way then no one is excused from the exercise. Everyone has their story, from the mere babes of the Kingdom to the wise and learned of this world. This book is an attempt to *do* theology, that is, to talk about God, from human experience.

Such an approach is not new. In fact, this method has its roots in the early Church. The Christian community spoke of and worshipped God as they *experienced* him/her in everyday individual and community life. The early Church and subsequent tradition has chosen to speak of the One God from a Trinity of experience. God is Creator, Redeemer, and Creative Presence. In more traditional language, God is Father, Son, and Spirit. The Trinitarian insight concerning God was first and essentially an experience and only later became a dogma or creed. For many today God is dead or absent or indifferent to our world and everyday concerns. God is not only a word that is false, it has become a word without *meaning*. The method of science cannot or will not find "proof" for God's existence; therefore, God must be dead as Nietzsche proclaimed. Technology and the "will to power" are what run our everyday world and not grace which seems so magical and unenlightened. Such a worldview cannot be easily dismissed. The daily paper and our everyday experience can challenge the most resolute believer that if God is not dead, he/she must be on a holiday. Yet, the contention of this book and the Christian symbol system is that our God cares and is not only with us but in Jesus God is *for* us. It is in the crosses and the darkness as much as in the resurrections and light that we experience our God. God is found in the marrow of life; *all* of life. God seeks us out and invites us to realize the possibilities of our humanness and experience the unboundedness of Divine Love.

This book owes its alpha and omega to so many, but a special word of gratitude is extended to Sister Grace Pilon, SBS. Sister Grace is the foundress of the educational system called Workshop Way, and through her encouragement this book has been made a reality. Thanks to Mrs. Freda Faber who cheerfully typed the manuscript. Finally, my gratitude is expressed to the faith communities of Xavier University of Louisiana and Mercy Academy of New Orleans for their support and openness.

Rev. William F. Maestri
New Orleans, 1980

PART I
God with Us

God Our Father

AS we begin our inquiry about God and the experience of Christian living it is essential to remember we do so with humility and contrition. All of our talk about God is symbolic and limited. Protestant theologian Paul Tillich wrote and preached about "the God beyond God". By this he meant that the God who is, and not the God of religion, is the One we worship. Tillich felt that we too often fall victim to an idolatry of ideas in which we worship the words or doctrine rather than the Really Real they attempt to explain. Therefore, our God-talk is done with a sense of contrition in that we always do injustice to the Reality we proclaim. We always fall short of God's glory. As Father John Shea observes, the orthodox position is the least offensive way of speaking about God.

Does this mean we should keep silent about God? Are we better off saying nothing? At times silence can be golden and our words can conceal as well as reveal. However, we are called to proclaim what God has done for us. It is through words and speech, however limited and imperfect, that we communicate and grow as individuals. Tillich is not asking us to refrain from speaking about God. He is asking us to do it with a needed sense of our creatureliness. We must speak about God in images we develop from human experience.

The Israelites spoke about Yahweh as Lord, Ruler, King, and various other images and titles taken from their experience of Yahweh. Above all they experienced Yahweh in personal terms, that is Yahweh as a "Thou". Their God was not impersonal, a principle of fertility, or some capricious despot. Rather, Yahweh was the God who created the universe and brought them into existence as a people. Furthermore, their God was a faithful God who established a covenant and a lasting bond with them. Yahweh could become angry and jealous. This was especially true when they chased after other gods. But Yahweh always remained faithful and always sought his people out when they went astray. God would not give up on them. The Israelites knew God loved them for Yahweh had revealed his Law to no other people. Yahweh chose them to be the instrument of his will in history. It is through them that the salvation of the world is to be realized. However, the depth of the Divine Love was not known until Yahweh took on a human face. The love of Yahweh is so deep it becomes one, totally and completely, with the one loved. God in Jesus is "true man of true man". The God of Love becomes one with us.

The request by the disciples to Jesus concerning prayer is crucial. They are really asking how they are to call God. In what way are they to address him? Much to their surprise and delight Jesus tells them to call God their "daddy". At first this may seem disrespectful. How could God be called such an irreverent name? Yet, that is what Jesus says. The Aramaic word Jesus uses is "abba". The closest English translation is "daddy". This name indicates a relationship with God of affection and love like the love relationship in a good family. Yahweh does not want our fear, burnt offerings, or compulsive obedience. Yahweh wants of us what "daddies" want for their children: happeness and the using of talents to the best of our ability. Yahweh wants our love and wants us to love and serve one another. If the truth be known, Yahweh is quite demanding. To give God our fear or an external show of reverence is easy. Yahweh wants more—he wants us completely. Our heart of stone must become a heart of flesh fashioned in his likeness.

If this transformation of heart or spirit is to take place we must learn to trust God and each other. In our own age this is not easy. We are children of Vietnam and Watergate. We have lost our child-like innocence. Authority cannot be trusted for it seeks its own ends and power. Authority does *not* have a human face. In our "mass society" authority and power are without identity or concern for us. Such is the conventional wisdom. Therefore, how can we trust and be open to God who seems so absent? How can we believe one another in a world that glorifies "the sting"? It is to these questions we now turn our attention.

Who Do You Trust?

THE famous psychiatrist, Erik Erikson, has described eight stages in the development of human personality. The first and most crucial of these stages is what Erikson calls basic trust. The child experiences his or her environment as safe and receptive to life. Basic needs are satisfied and the child experiences an overall feeling of well-being. If this stage of basic trust is not experienced or severely hampered the effects continue throughout the other seven stages. Basic trust is essential to human growth.

Before Johnny Carson and Ed McMahon became late night fixtures on the *Tonight Show*, they teamed together on an afternoon quiz show entitled *Who Do You Trust?* The Scriptures ask us the same question: Who do you trust? Israel has always had an ambivalent relationship with Yahweh. Yahweh was their creator and the one who saved them. The Hebrew prophets often spoke of Israel's relationship with Yahweh in terms of a marriage convenant. Like any good marriage the relationship was spiced with love and hate; tenderness and indifference; sadness and joy. Israel is not above chasing the latest idol or fad in the Biblical version of "keeping up with the Baals". Israel at times sought political security with other nations rather than the trusting covenant relationship with Yahweh. The prophet must continue to remind, threaten, encourage, and challenge the people to turn to Yahweh in trust.

Jesus continues this fundamental theme in his preaching and ministry: God is your loving Father who cares and wants what is best for his people. Jesus is saying that God must be the focus and center of our life. In the terminology of Paul Tillich, God must be our "ultimate concern". God alone is the ground of all human concerns and loves. God is the all-encompassing horizon who gives meaning to all of life. God is the Love through whom all other loves find purpose and bear fruit.

Today we are encouraged to trust and believe only that which we produce. Trust and faith and love have lost their vertical dimension. We trust our money, the Gross National Product, the military and industrial complex, our powers of consumption and production, and above all, we place an unquestioning trust in technology. If Assyria and the Golden Calf could not save Israel, why is it that technology should fare any better? Is not the question of redemption and peace as old as humankind itself? Is not humankind's flirtation with the finite as the answer to our basic incompleteness just as old and inadequate? The answer to the fundamental restlessness we all experience is expressed powerfully in the Book of Deuteronomy: we are to love God with our whole being. It is God alone in whom we place our ultimate trust and make our ultimate concern. To love God ultimately is to place our entire being in the mysterious presence of, and to be open to, his creative word.

To make God our ultimate concern is not to destroy the concerns of our everyday existence. God is the ultimate concern who enriches and gives meaning to our finite concerns. Our everyday does not become less real, but becomes part of the Really Real; not less free, but more liberated in love of God and service to our neighbor; not despairing, but with God as our ultimate concern, the everyday is enriched, blessed, transformed, and finally redeemed. The banality, routine, struggles, the profane aspects of the everyday—in effect our crosses—become united with the Cross of the Crucified and Risen Lord. The Christian life continues to ask the fundamental question—who do *you* trust? The answer comes from our everyday existence.

God Calls Us by Name

ONE of the most fundamental questions we must all ask and answer concerns what we believe the nature of reality to be. Do we believe life to be absurd and without meaning, and therefore one must live for the moment and oneself? Or, do we believe that there is meaning and purpose to life, and above all, each of us makes a "real difference" in the world? Our response depends greatly on our life experiences, training and image of God. The pages of Scripture, however, are clear on this point: individual and social life has meaning and purpose, and Yahweh is a God who cares. God creates out of love and calls all reality to share the divine life. Yahweh is not distant but he knows us and calls us by name.

The notion of "being called by name" is written on every page of Scripture. It is Yahweh who calls forth creation in its richness and complexity. Yahweh places man in trustful stewardship over the work of his hands. Humankind has been crowned "with glory and is a little less than the angels". The call of Yahweh is a spoken word that is active and life-giving. The word of the Lord demands a response from the one addressed. One can never remain indifferent from an

encounter with the Ancient One. The fact that
Yahweh addresses his creation and people is
testimony to the fundamental fact of relationship. Life is not to be experienced in loneliness
or indifference, but in openness and trust. This
can be done with confidence since the "Ground
of Being" is fundamentally related to all of life.

In the words of Scripture, "in the fullness of
time God sent his only Son," that is, God spoke
his definitive Word in time and in our human
condition. In so doing, God forever committed
himself to us and the world. In Jesus, the full expression of God's presence, all creation is called
to join in the Wedding Feast of the Kingdom of
God. This definitive of God's Word is not a once
only utterance. God continues to renew and
reconcile all of creation to himself. Jesus is still
with us through the working of the Holy Spirit.
This abiding presence of the Spirit is located in
the Church as the visible reminder of God's love
for the world. The "last days" of the prophet Joel
have dawned in Christ. The Spirit is being
poured out on all flesh and waiting in eager longing for the Lord's return in his fullness.

The Latin word *Vocāre* means "to call". Our
word vocation is so derived. All of us have a
vocation or call from God to enrich the world
and daily life by our presence. God's word is active in our lives and calling forth a response
from us. God calls each of us by name for a particular work to do. God searches our heart and

knows us. So intimate is his knowledge of us that "the hairs on our head are counted". Each of us is called individually by name. The word of the Lord comes in a particular, concrete way in our lives. There is no general or abstract call as there is no genuine love in the abstract. Love and God's call are concrete and specific.

Our vocation begins with Baptism, is nourished by the Eucharist, and continues throughout our life until we return to our Father's home. Even after our earthly existence we continue to grow and be enriched by God's life. So far we have said that God is our Creator and Father who loves and cares for us. Our God is one who wants to share the very depth of his love with us. Yahweh is the one in whom we place our trust and who is our ultimate concern. However, God so loved us that he made us free. Love and freedom can never be separated. Genuine love as a human response demands genuine freedom. God wants our response to love, but only a response that is freely given. Humankind can and has abused freedom and failed to trust and love God ultimately. In other words, humankind knows the destructive presence of sin. In our day, however, sin and its effects have been somewhat forgotten. Many wonder what sin is, anyway and if modern humankind has not outgrown such a category. It is on sin and our everyday experience we must now focus our attention.

Sin?

THE word sin has caused much confusion and misunderstanding. We tend, in frustration, to dismiss it as a reality. Sin is often looked upon as a ridiculous aspect of some outdated religious superstition. Sin is an affront to our human dignity. Often sin appears simply as a negative command telling us not to do what we most want to do. Psychiatrist Karl Menninger wrote a book entitled, *Whatever Became of Sin?*. Dr. Menninger wonders aloud if modern humankind has lost its sense of sin. He asks a crucial question. For it implies that we take seriously and we accept responsibility for our actions and our failure to act. Only an adult or an adult "in process" can seriously ask this question.

The question before us deserves our utmost attention: Can anyone sin anymore? The answer is YES. However, this yes needs development. Sin is not only a list of don'ts; we need to examine the experience of sin in the singular as it affects each of us and our world. St. Paul does not speak of sins in the plural as some list of Divine Don'ts, but he speaks of sin as a power and force woven into the very marrow of our existence. Sin is fundamentally the experience of separation, alienation and estrangement. Sin is a statement of *being* before it is a statement of *action*. Sin is the revelation of *who* we are before it is *what* we have done or not done. Sin and guilt call us to recognize our true condition before God and our fellow human beings. The experience of sin is felt in three basic ways.

1. *Separation from others.* Who has not experienced loneliness in the midst of a party, meeting, family gathering or some social event? It is almost as if the greater the noise and talk the deeper our feeling of separation. Why is this so? Life has within it a fundamental element of separation. The deepest love and the most intimate moments of human revelation are never fully complete. We hold back and remain a basic mystery to the other. Not only do we experience the separation of life on an individual level, but more especially on a social level. The separation of nations, generations, races, classes, and religions indicates how conscious we are of that which divides us rather than that which unites us. We can sit in the comfort of our homes, watch the TV news, eat a meal and feel little or nothing for the victims of violence and tragedy. We may feel a momentary shock but we soon return to our "normal" routine. We sleep well. Life is separated from life.

2. *Estrangement from the self.* Not only are others a mystery to us, but we are a mystery and puzzle to ourselves. Often we do not understand our own thoughts, feelings, and actions. Often we do the very things that hurt us and our loved ones. Feelings of inadequacy, unworthiness, and inferiority come over us for no particular reason. How often do we think, say, and do things, that on reflection, shock us? We surprise ourselves and we often cannot believe our own behavior. Such existential surprise is not new. St. Paul in his letter to the Romans (Chapter 7) experienced the same feeling. He called it the "war within himself" and the result of sin. His life was in conflict and filled with a desperate longing for inner peace. Who will save him (and us) and overcome this basic estrangement? The Lord Jesus Christ. Until the Lord comes in his fullness we groan inwardly and pray, "Come Lord Jesus."

3. *Alienation from God.* We are separated from others, estranged from the self, and we are alienated from God. Through sin we become a stranger to the ground and source of life. In our heart of hearts we know that we are made for greatness. There is a call deep within us, but our ears are closed, our eyes swollen shut with pride, and our hearts are like cold stones. We rebel against the God who speaks to our spirit.

We are alienated from God and our true home. Every happiness is fleeting; every victory soon passes into defeat; and every joy passes away. We all experience the inner restlessness and desperation that the things of this world cannot satisfy. This existential uneasiness can be quieted by God alone, who is our peace.

The Catholic tradition has spoken not only of sin but also of sins. It must be remembered that there are few new sins. What is needed is an examination of the new ways of committing old sins. The best available list is the Ten Commandments. The Commandments offer us a wide variety of attitudes and behavior patterns by which we can judge *our* life. The Ten Commandments are guidelines to authentic, moral living. The Ten Commandments are concerned with two broad areas of relationship: God and neighbor. The Commandments call us to be on guard against carving idols out of money, status, class, and intelligence. We can fashion idols by forming a false image of God as one who is vengeful and punishing. Also we are challenged to be reverent toward God's name and the work of His hands in creation. God calls us to make holy the Sabbath. But not only the Sabbath, each day is a day of holiness and a challenge to worship and honor God.

We are not only in relationship with God, but

we are related to others. The Commandments forbid acts of violence by word, deed, or attitude. They call us to respect authority figures just as they call for authority figures to respect those they lead and serve. We are to deal with each other in an honest and sincere way. This means we must respect the rights of others and deal with our neighbor in a spirit of truth and integrity. In the age of the "rip-off" and the "sting" we are called to respect the property of others. Finally, the sixth and ninth Commandments call us to examine the quality of our relationship and see if fidelity, love, and commitment are alive and present. These Commandments are not only, or even chiefly, sexual. The quality of our relationships in *all aspects* is crucial to the Christian life.

What we have said to date is that there *is* sin and *there are* sins. Both can lead to death if we misuse our freedom and decide to live for ourselves alone. We can decide to close off the lure of God and withdraw from others. We can fix all our energies on the self alone. Sin is not, however, the entire story of our condition. We not only experience sin and slavery, but also freedom. Freedom is our curse, it is also our greatness. Just what is freedom anyway?

Freedom's Creed

VICTOR HUGO was fond of reminding his audience that nothing was more powerful than an idea whose time has come. In our own age the idea which carries such force is freedom. Americans are in love with freedom. Freedom is the cornerstone of our political system. Personal liberty has been won at a dear price—the lives of untold numbers who believed that life without freedom was not worth living. Independence is our birthright and we will die to defend it. Yet, we must ask what seems to be a rather absurd question: Do we really want freedom? Let us not be too quick to answer. We may end up disappointed, like the rich young man who wished to follow Jesus *until* he heard what was required.

The late French existentialist philosopher Jean Paul Sartre's view of the human condition is one in which freedom is the only absolute norm of conduct. Man is the freedom-animal who must decide about him or herself each moment in the process of forming one's essence. In the chilling words of Sartre, "Man is condemned to be free." What a strange way to put it: freedom and condemnation. Yet, Sartre knows well the vast majority prefer to live in bad faith.

That is, the majority of humankind prefer to hand over ownership of the self to others, to institutions, or tradition for formation and decision. The majority find freedom an awesome burden; a millstone around the neck. The radical (root) freedom of Sartre's philosophy demands radical *responsibility*. We cannot escape the task of self-formation and the judgment, as authentic or inauthentic, that follows. We cannot blame others, our genes, parents, environment, or even the most powerful of all influences—the Zodiac. We cannot explain away responsibility for who we are and what we do by saying, "my sign crossed over into the wrong moon or house and settled in a rather bad orbit." Long before Sartre, Shakespeare reminded us, "the trouble lies not in the stars but in ourselves." Psychiatrist Erich Fromm is of the opinion that most people want to "escape from freedom". The rise of totalitarian governments witnesses to the desire to be well kept, fed, clothed, and above all, told what to do. Life ceases to be examined and thoughtful. No doubt Socrates would add, "and not with living too." Certainly such a life is inauthentic and lacks zest.

The well-kept existence that seeks security at all cost is not what God expects of us. Freedom is a fundamental gift of our human condition. As such, this gift is to be used and nurtured. We cannot bury it in the ground because we are afraid of what we or others might do with it. God is big enough and trusting enough, as is any good parent, to suffer our mistakes and sins and still love us. God suffers our immaturity in expressing our love and freedom. God lures us to new levels of intensity and novelty. This growth process is only possible to the extent that we exercise our freedom.

At the heart of the Biblical witness concerning freedom is the contention that freedom and obedience are inter-related and not opposites. To experience real freedom, the freedom that comes from truth, calls for a maturity on our part—a maturity that demands *decentralization*. We become less and less so God can become more and more the center of our lives. In the process of this spiritual discipline we discover a great truth: as God becomes more and more the center of life, we become more and more authentic and alive. We experience the authentic liberation—freedom to love God and serve our neighbor. We experience freedom *from* compulsive drives for power and material security. We become free *for* others knowing that God, our Father, knows what we need before we ask. This same loving God pours gifts a hundredfold into our hearts.

Roots

IN the previous pages we spoke about freedom and the importance of the responsible use of our freedom. The responsible use of freedom continues to be one of the most serious challenges to personal and group existence. It is not enough that we are free, we must always examine what we are free *for*, and how we choose to exercise our freedom. The responsible use of freedom is not easy, as the history of humankind so vividly indicates. In fact, if we return to the beginning we see that early on in the development of humankind, freedom was irresponsibly used. Chapters two and three in the Book of Genesis call us to meditate upon our origins. This is the story of our roots and beginnings. Still, it is hard to imagine any more offensive selections in Scripture than these. The creation stories in Genesis are an affront to the modern mind. Why is this so?

These chapters remind us of our position and responsibility in the cosmos: that is, each of us is a *creature*. Our creatureliness means that we are dependent, beholden to someone or something, and above all, we are finite and temporal. We pass away and are no more. To be a creature is to acknowledge how contingent is our existence and how fragile our life. The stories in Genesis remind us also that we are not just any creature, but we are made in the image and likeness of God. We are creatures with responsibility who have been entrusted with a stewardship over God's handiwork. To acknowledge our creatureliness is also to evoke the feeling of gratitude for all that we have received and all that we are.

One could still persist and say, "Yes, we are creatures, dependent, contingent, and share responsibility for the world. So what?" Humankind in our present epoch is held under the sway of science and its application through technology. We live under the illusion that we are the *creator* and no longer the creature. We live with the illusion that everything that is, is the result of our efforts and genius. In the words of William Barrett, we live under the "illusion of technique". All of reality is reduced to the work of our hands alone. Life is one-dimensional. The windows of the cosmos have been closed. The situation for modern man is cosmic and existential loneliness. Man is the one and only of his kind. There is no relationship to a reality beyond or a connection with life below. Man is on his own.

There is a great danger present in such a situation. It is the danger that we will come, if we have not already, to regard ourselves as absolute masters of all reality. The image of humankind today is that of the engineer, manipulator, and great controller. The influence of our engineering and manipulating is most keenly felt in our relationship to nature. The present ecological situation indicates how well or how poorly we have managed that relationship. The image of man as engineer has not stopped with nature, but in this century man the engineer has become man the engineered. The most profound of all revolutions has dawned— man is the project to be created by man in his own genetic image and likeness.

The desire of modern man to dominate nature has led to man's increased domination and control over his fellow man. This is not new to history. What is new and frightening is the degree of effectiveness through technology, and the large numbers of people living in totalitarian forms of government. However, even in the so-called free countries, technology in the hands of advertisers and media experts controls large segments of the population's taste, values, and general world-view. An important question is whether the media reports the news or *makes* the news? Modern man, the technocrat, has become intoxicated with his power. However, one must wonder if we have acquired the necessary wisdom to use such power for human well-being. We continue to "darken our world" with the thirst for atomic power in the balance of terror. We continue to squander our resources and rape our environment. Our technological arrogance has been carried into the lab in the fabrication of life through genetic manipulation.

What are we to do and how are we to live? We cannot and should not advocate a return to some idyllic past which in reality never existed. The nostalgic romanticism which looks to the past for truth and ideals is just as ineffective as the utopian visionary who trivializes the past and present in search for a perfect tomorrow. Such a tomorrow will not be ours short of the Kingdom of God. What is needed is a genuine conversion or *metanoia*. We need to re-open the horizon of our being for God's grace. We need to be open in spirit and truth to his healing word and grace. This conversion process will only begin when we reclaim our creatureliness, not as an insult, but for what it really is—proof of God's love for us. This conversion calls for a change in our intellectual horizon in which we again make space for the sacred and holy in our daily existence. It is our task and greatness to prepare a way for God's reappearance in our world. We are called to re-learn our dignity as child of God and co-creator in the world. We cannot "go it alone" because we grow only in relationship with God and others. This is a hard lesson for us to learn, we who live "East of Eden". The words of Augustine 1500 years ago still have "cash value" today: "Let man first learn what it means to be man before man learns what it is to be God. For when man learns what it means to be man, he will not want to be God."

East of Eden

EACH of us is meant for greatness from the moment of our birth to the hour of our death. Greatness is part of the marrow of our bones. We are made in God's image and called to grow into his likeness. At the end of our earthly existence we are to hand back to our Father what he first gave us—life. God is with us at the beginning, middle, end and beyond of existence. God has called us to be stewards of his creation and in responsible freedom to respond to him in love. However, we all know that something went wrong with the game plan. We got the characters and lives confused. We thought life something to be grasped and freedom a mere expression of the ego's will to power. In so doing we fell from grace and became estranged from God and all creation. History serves as a testimony to what a paradox we are: greatness and smallness; nobility and pettiness; light and darkness. Our origin is Eden, but we cannot go home again. We are citizens of the earth and we make our abode East of Eden. Yet we know that we are strangers and pilgrims. The call of greatness is always present even in a world that pollutes our eyes and deafens us with the hum of the machine. Eden is gone. Earth is transitory.

Maestri

Our true home is the present and future Kingdom of God. A Kingdom that is among us and within us, and at the same time is ahead of us in the future. The Kingdom of God stands in opposition to the multitudinous Towers of Babel humankind has fashioned for itself.

Today many people believe that many, if not all, of our problems could be solved if only we communicated better. The conflict between the generations, races, economic and religious groups, even nations, would cease with better communication. We need to speak the same language and be on the same wavelength. A corollary to this "bliss through better communications" is the belief that through technological and cultural advances, humankind can become the New Being. Given enough time and sufficient effort and money, humankind can build the new Jerusalem here on earth. If we try to separate these two choice morsels of conventional wisdom, we find that what was thought to be prime filet turns out to be horse meat!

The Book of Genesis recounts the first Babel and human history pays tragic testimony to all of its offspring. Humankind communicates *too well*. There is only one language and the vocabulary so simple everyone can learn it. But something goes amiss. They (and we as well) are communicating East of Eden. The problem lies not in the language or communication techniques, but rather, the trouble lies in the heart of humankind. The scene has shifted from Eden, but the story is the same—pride and the arrogant over-extension of human willfulness. Whether one wants to be like the gods, as in Eden, or build a tower and reach the gods, the desire is the same. Humankind wants to be what it is not. In the effort to be more we become less. This is the essence of the Fall. It is not a place as much as it is a condition of estrangement and falling away from our true peace and blessedness.

Until we recognize the limitations of our human condition and the source of our true greatness, we will continue to know tragedy. We all live East of Eden and journey toward God's Kingdom. Technological man is really the image of humankind throughout history and not one beginning just in the sixteenth century. Man the builder, doer, and engineer is present with Babel. The Babel mentality is alive and well, thank you, in our own time. We are still searching with longing hearts for peace and that which endures beyond the reign of death. We are searching for that mystery who is "ever old and ever new," who creates, redeems, and lures us to our true greatness. This is the miracle of daily life and the mystery of the everyday. In the ordinary and routine demands of each day we find God and our authentic self.

Miracles

MIRACLES are a lot like us and our human relationships: we expect too much and receive too little and are often misunderstood. In terms of expectations we look for miracles in the flashy and spectacular. Miracles are supposed to be the great interruptions in our everyday lives and stand the laws of nature on their collective heads. To be a miracle of any note the Red Sea must part; the dead rise; the lame learn to jog; and the blind regain their sight. Miracles are the "big events" and the stuff we can't ignore.

However, we must realize how much this view of miracles has gotten us into trouble. The "cutting edge" of miracles today, and certainly for the past 200 years, has been on the decline. The British philosopher, David Hume, believed miracles were an insult to the modern mind and an obstacle to truth. Today we cut our teeth on science and technology and find miracles difficult to come by. There is a deep irony present: miracles were meant to be a help to faith, however, they have come to be seen as a stumbling block to growth. Much of the blame for this general disrepute attributed to miracles is due to our ill-founded miracle-talk.

The God for Every Day

The understanding of miracles as a spectacular suspension of reason and the everyday workings of nature ought to die; and the quicker the better. This is *not* to say miracles ought to die. In fact, I would suggest that miracles are alive and well. What we need is a new understanding of miracles. Miracles are something you see everyday. They are smaller than a breadbox. And some of your best friends just might be miracles. The pages of Scripture bring home to us the importance of the ordinary and everyday things that fill our lives. It is the taken-for-granted and common that holds the mysteries of existence. It is in the everyday with its familiarity and routine, boredom and banality, that we find the hidden but ever present reality of the Holy. The challenge is for us to see deeply and with wisdom.

Miracles are often the quiet and ordinary moments of God's grace and revelation in our daily lives. Everyday miracles are beautiful days and clear, cold winter nights. Miracles are a child's laughter and the pain that comes to the young who must struggle with increased freedom and responsibility. They are flowers and clouds and rain. Miracles are present and made visible through human beings who commit themselves to ideals such as justice, love and peace. Miracles are present when and where men and women confront the age-old enemies of humankind—ignorance, poverty, and disease. Miracles are present in the depth of our sorrow and brokenness when healing and reconciliation begin to occur.

In an age when "small is beautiful," "less is more," and "the free ride is over," we need to lower our expectations, but not our hopes or vision. Big miracles still come now and then. But more often than not we see them in the inner strength exhibited by a Pope who comes with no army or worldly power save the power of love and the Spirit of Jesus. He touches our hearts and opens our eyes to new possibilities of being-in-the-world. He comes proclaiming the power of love and an enduring belief in the human spirit. He comes as a man of hope in the name of the One who is our hope. Millions stop and *listen*, and that is a true miracle!

Waiting

WILLIAM SOMERSET MAUGHAM once wrote
that the three most difficult things for humans to
endure were to be in bed and sleep not; try to
please and please not; and wait for one who
comes not. We might add, "and the most difficult of these is waiting." Ours is a society that
is obsessed with the instant. We want what we
want and we want it now if not sooner. The time
imperative that structures our everyday is the
fast—and faster still. Our technology has
delivered us an instant world: from instant-on
TV, to instant food, to even instant-on relationships with the help of computer dates. We have
instant communication with any part of the
world. The eye of the camera and the voice of
the radio place us in contact with the far cor-
ners of the earth. The world is our village and
we are no longer insulated from world tragedy
(Cambodia, Guyana) or world hope (the election
of a new pope). And yet, strange as it seems,
never have so many felt alienated and alone.
Our fabricated world has cut us off from the
rhythms of nature and the flow of seasons. Time
is strapped to our wrist and calculated into
demanding, often dehumanizing, schedules.

How often do we feel more driven than driving? With all of our power to control, how often do we feel controlled and manipulated?

In our everyday experience we find it so annoying to wait. We are impatient in car lines, grocery lines, and fast food lines which never quite live up to our expectations. How often after a day of work and hurrying do we fall into a chair and sigh, "I seem to be in a constant hurry to go nowhere"? Our lives are lived under the demon of the instant and we seem to be ruled by Freud's Pleasure Principle. That is, we cannot tolerate any delay in our gratification and enjoyment. We want our "kicks" so we turn to "speed," alcohol, and permissive sex in order to cope and find pleasurable escapes. Yet, we know that waiting is essential to growth. However, not only is waiting difficult but a greater challenge is knowing what to wait for. All of our waiting is done so as to bring us peace, happiness, and inner harmony. So often we wait for the wrong thing, or we wait for that which is only a temporal good which we have raised to the ultimate. Power, sex, popularity, reputation, and worldly wisdom are often proposed for our peace and happiness. If only I can amass enough money I can rest in peace. If only we can build more bombs than the Russians we will be secure. If only I can improve my sexual attractiveness I will be valuable as a human being. If only I am accepted by everyone I can accept myself. The list is endless. But even if we accomplished all of these we would still live what Emerson called "lives of quiet desperation." For if our waiting is based on the passing glories and goods of this world we are doomed to final disappointment. The desire for peace and happiness will not, in the last analysis, take root in our hearts. Our hearts will only know existential weariness.

The Scriptures speak to us of a weariness, not only of a physical sort, but a deep weariness of the heart. It is a weariness that Dante described as the "middle course of life". It is a world weariness. Such weariness is experienced by those whose hearts are burdened and heavy laden. The healing needed for such a condition is found only in God who is our peace. This peace of God is for those who least expect it, demand it, or even deserve it. The peace of God comes ultimately to those who wait even in the midst of what seems to be his silence, indifference, or death. God's refreshing presence comes to those who are bruised by life and exhausted in the struggle to live more authentically. God's refreshment comes to those who run the race of life; fight the good fight of faith; and persevere to the end. It comes especially to those who feel the burden of guilt and lack of acceptance. In the midst of our deep self-questioning and the anxiety as to whether life has meaning, God's grace-filled presence comes and reaffirms those who struggle in difficult circumstances and feel no support or recognition for their work. God is with those who struggle daily with doubt about God and cry from their depth, "I believe Lord. Help my unbelief."

To be human is to be world-weary and discontented. We wait and grow weary with a world that finds so little room for him who created all out of love. Waiting causes us tension. We can't help but wonder if we won't be disappointed again. Another hope turns to despair. In the midst of our weariness and doubt, Isaiah's words are for us:

> He gives power to the faint,
> and to him who has no might he increases
>   strength . . .
> they who wait for the Lord shall renew
>   their strength,
> they shall mount up with wings like eagles,
> they shall run and not be weary,
> they shall walk and not faint.

A profound vision indeed. Our hearts skip a beat and we cry out, "Come Lord Jesus."

PART II
God for Us

The Divine Love

THE Old Testament speaks to us in powerful ways and images of God's love for his people and creation. However, the Divine Love is always presented as a "second-order" activity. That is, God's love is mediated through such secondary causes as the prophets, mighty deeds in history such as the Exodus, and through natural phenomena (dreams). God's love and presence were always one step removed from the human. No one could see the face of God and live. Even Moses had to speak with Yahweh through the burning bush. The Old Testament, nonetheless, speaks of God's love for his covenanted people. The Israelites are his and he will use them as a blessing for all the nations. The Divine Love is universal and seeks to draw all things to it. But no matter how eloquent the Old Testament witness to God's love, this love was always removed to some degree. The Israelites and all creation longed for the day when the Divine Love and Will would be revealed in its fullness. The hope of the ages was for the complete restoration of God, humankind, and the world. Finally, "in the fullness of time" a new epoch dawned. The depth of the Divine Love and Will became visi-

ble. The Ancient One who dwells in unapproachable light truly shines in the darkness
and brings the eternal Light of Life. The
transcendent, all-powerful, judge, ruler, and
king Yahweh reveals the Divine Nature—
Unbounded Love in the child Jesus. God takes a
"human face" and so we experience not only
God with us but now God is *for* us. In Jesus, God
makes the ultimate love commitment to humankind and the world.

Scripture scholars tell us that we can approach the New Testament from two basic
theological perspectives: the Paschal Mystery
and the Incarnation. The Paschal Mystery
centers on the passion, death, and resurrection
of Christ. Jesus is the "Suffering Servant" of
Yahweh who becomes the innocent victim
through whom our guilt and sins are removed.
By his sufferings we are made whole. Through
his stripes we are healed and can become the
"new creature". The Paschal Mystery and its
effects on humankind and the world are
predominant in the Pauline writings.

The other perspective is termed "Incarnation". Such a view centers on the *Logos* or Word
of God entering our history and human condition. In so doing, a new Genesis or new beginning
takes place. In the Word becoming flesh the
decisive corner in history is turned and
humankind is invited to eternal life. The In-

carnational perspective lies at the heart of the Johannine writings. This approach has much to offer us concerning Christian existence. Let us meditate on just two aspects: the fundamental goodness of human existence, and secondly, the need for fraternal love to be the grounding principle of all interpersonal relationships.

The Danish philosopher Soren Kierkegaard called the Incarnation the "Ultimate Paradox" of history which could only be accepted by a "leap of faith". The Omnipotent and Wholly Other God assumed our condition and became one like us so as to be for us. St. John tells us the motive for such a paradox: "God so loved the world that he sent his only Son, not to condemn the world, but to save the world" (Jn. 3:16f). God creates and recreates out of the Divine Nature which is Divine Love. It is out of love that God assumes our condition and accepts it and brings it to full measure. The Incarnation is not God becoming less, but is humankind being offered the possibility of becoming what it was truly meant to be. The Incarnation is not the negation of the human, but its fulfillment and perfection. God has accepted our human condition in its completeness and challenges us to accept ourselves. Jesus is the challenge and possibility of calling God our Father and living each day doing the will of our Father. The Incarnation is the ultimate testimony that God's creation and especially humankind, is good and loved by God.

The Incarnational approach to Christian existence is a definite commitment to community. Even when Jesus returns to the glory of his Father the disciples are not left orphans. The Paraclete guides them in forming a community life grounded in love. But not just any notion of love will do. The distinguishing mark of the Christian and the community is the love Jesus expressed and challenged them *to do*. Love is an action word. The Christian community is to love one another as Jesus loved them. Such a Jesus-like love is faithful and sacrificial. There are even instances in which such a love demands the ultimate: the laying down of one's life for the brethren. Each Christian community is called to be a sign and living reminder of the depth of the Divine Love. In other words, each community by its love life *continues* the Incarnation in history. Each community continues to speak to the world of God's love and God's invitation to realize its true destiny.

Jesus is the one in whom God and man meet in the great process of reconciliation. The understanding of Jesus as *both* God and man is not first and foremost the result of Greek philosophy, but is primarily the result of the disciple's *experience* of Jesus. To be sure, there were other holy men and women who spoke the Lord's word and did his will. There were many pious folk during Jesus' time who longed for the Messiah. But in Jesus people experienced something unique and special. Jesus taught and spoke about God and human possibilities in a new way. Jesus spoke with authority and a conviction. Jesus spoke about God as the loving Father of all his children. Above all, Jesus offered those who responded in faith the opportunity to experience the Divine Life. God was the Really Real, so much so, that the Christian community could say that God was in Jesus, and ultimately, God and Jesus are one and the same. The experience of Jesus as "true God of true God" was given formal expression with the Council of Nicea (325 A.D.). We must, however, be careful not to disvalue the humanity of Jesus which the Council of Chalcedon (451 A.D.) confirmed ("true man of true man"). We cannot afford to lose either of these in our Jesus-talk.

It is worth noting that the earliest gospel was written by St. Mark sometime between 60 and 70 A.D. Mark, the evangelist (one who proclaims a good news), is mentioned several times in the New Testament. The primary source for Mark's gospel was Peter, although he did use other pre-existing materials in his narrative. Mark's style is lacking in literary polish or sophistication. He uses a large number of colloquialisms and the overall vocabulary is quite limited. So far I have given you what American philosophers would call the "stubborn and irreducible facts" concerning Mark and his gospel. Why did Mark write a gospel?—and secondly, how does Mark paint Jesus?

As to why Mark wrote his gospel we can offer the following speculations. Mark wanted to preserve the authentic memory and teaching of Jesus. This was very important for two reasons: the inner circle of eye-witnesses to the historical Jesus were dying off, and secondly, the Way was being preached beyond Jerusalem and coming in contact with different cultures and religious beliefs. Mark wanted to safeguard the vision of Jesus from contamination and heresy. But more important than doctrinal purity, Mark's gospel is an act of faith written for those in the faith. Mark is not writing a modern historical biography. He is not the cold, detached scholar fitting the pieces together. Mark is a man committed to Jesus whom he proclaims as God's Son. Mark is writing about someone whom he loves and has faith in. Jesus is the Son of God who proclaims the Kingdom, suffers and dies, only to rise three days later.

Mark is an artist and is grasped by a vision that must be told. The gospel is the canvas onto which he paints his picture of Jesus. And what a beautiful picture it is. Mark paints Jesus in real flesh and blood colors. Jesus is God's Son to be sure, but he is completely human too. Jesus is the carpenter who works. The miracles of Jesus depend on the faith of the receiver, and sometimes the miracles need a second try (blind man). Jesus forbids anyone to call him good, for God alone is good. He is ignorant of certain things. Jesus suffers rejection, misunderstanding, and hostility. Controversies and doubts swirl about him, even among his trusted circle of Twelve. Mark paints us a Jesus who cries, gets angry, hungers and thirsts, and grows weary. What is most important in Mark's portrait of Jesus is this: Mark was not afraid to proclaim a human Jesus. He did not believe one would think less of Jesus, be less religious, or less good, if Jesus shared in a total way our condition. That which endears Mark to us is precisely the fact that he gives us a Jesus, and a God, who are attractive and filled with the power of love. The human Jesus proclaims the Kingdom and moves the heart of humankind.

In today's world of Superstars, wonder women, and supermen, Mark has much to say to us about the beauty and power of being authentically human. Mark is saying to us that we need not be ashamed of our humanity. God does not love and accept us because of our ability to leap tall buildings, to speed faster than a bullet, or even write a book. God loves us simply because ... because we are his children and he wants us to develop our humanness. And isn't this the best good news possible?

The Divine Jesus

CHRISTIANS of every age are in Mark's debt for his good news about the human Jesus. Whenever we forget that Jesus is truly human Mark's gospel serves as a gentle reminder. However, the humanity of Jesus is not the total picture, and Mark would certainly agree. God was present totally and completely in the man Jesus so that one could say in Jesus God and man are one. We cannot speak of the humanity of Jesus without his divinity, and vice versa. In the previous section we spoke about the human Jesus. It is to the Jesus as "true God of true God" that we now direct our attention.

The divinity of Jesus was one of the most crucial controversies to face the early Church. How was it that the man Jesus was also God? There certainly was not agreement on this issue. A very learned cleric named Arius believed that Jesus was made or begotten from the Father. In effect, Jesus was created and did not pre-exist with the Father from all eternity. Jesus was the most perfect of creatures, but a creature nonetheless. The views of Arius were condemned. The Church turned to a bishop of Alexandria named Athanasius (295-373 A.D.). St. Atha-

Maestri

nasius put forward the term *homoousios*, that is, Jesus is consubstantial with the Father and not created by Him. Jesus is "true God of true God."

This controversy between Arius and Athanasius may at first blush seem merely to be nothing more than theological in-fighting. Yet there is more at stake. At the heart of Athanasius's theology is the blending of the person of Jesus as the Christ with the mission of Jesus as savior of the World. Jesus must be truly God so that humankind can participate in God's divine life. The redemption of the world is accomplished through the loving action of God becoming truly human and at the same time remaining God. In the words of St. Athanasius: "The Word of God became man that we might become God." The ultimate destiny of humankind is so much a part of God's life that man becomes divinized through the redemption process. The divine image is restored through the Incarnation and Paschal Mystery of Jesus. Athanasius is concerned to show that man had lost, through sin, the divine life and reconciliation could only be accomplished through the God-Man Jesus.

If the debate were held today between Arius and Athanasius, I suspect Athanasius would fare badly. In the age of Jesus Christ Superstar and Superman, with its obvious Christological overtones, it is Athanasius who would be ruled out of order, or worse, irrelevant. The Christological

58

pendulum has swung to the human side of Jesus. The present Christological climate favors the so-called "Christ from below" rather than the "Christ from above". In simpler terms, we want to accentuate Jesus' one-like-usness. This is certainly commendable and necessary. A God too distant becomes a God we soon learn to live without. We forget the too distant God because we believe that he has forgotten about us. I suspect much of the "Death of God theology" resulted from an over-emphasis on the transcendence of God. In a strange way the death of God theologians served a valuable purpose. They reminded us never to speak about the God above us without also speaking about the God within us.

It must be restated, however, that we cannot allow the humanity of Jesus to swallow up his divinity. If we overlook the divinity in Jesus, we overlook the divine in ourselves. We overlook an essential part of our being—the spiritual dimension. If we become too absorbed in the human, all too human, we can conceal the Spirit who dwells within. To see Jesus in only human terms runs the risk of making salvation a human achievement. If Jesus is human to the exclusion of the divine, then salvation is accomplished by one of us; the best of us to be sure, yet essentially one of us. Salvation is no longer a divine initiative and gift, but it is something we earn and have a right to. God owes us heaven. We have worked and paid our earthly dues. The toll-gate of paradise will open wide in acknowledgment of all *we have done*. How surprised we will be when Jesus informs us that life with him is not something we earn or can demand. Life with Jesus is a free gift and all we need is the courage to accept it and trust in the Lord.

The divinity of Jesus must be preserved as a constant reminder that we stand in reverence, awe, and gratitude before the mystery of Salvation. The crib and the cross are the ultimate testaments of God's love for each of us. The crib reveals the depth of the Divine Love. The cross stands on Calvary and casts its shadow over history and us as an eternal reminder that in Jesus, God and man meet. On the cross the human and the divine are forever one.

I've Got a Secret

THE tension between the humanity and divinity of Jesus was not just a concern for the early Church and academics. It concerned Jesus and Mark the evangelist. Not only does Mark paint a human Jesus, but the Jesus of Mark seems to be playing an ancient version of "I've Got a Secret". Biblical scholars refer to this coyness as the "Messianic Secret". Please don't be frightened away from reading further by the ominous term. It's really quite interesting.

Jesus frequently goes about healing or performing some miracle only to issue a stern warning to keep silent about the whole affair. Jesus even goes so far as to warn the demons to keep his identity a secret: "Mum's the word." Naturally we want to ask: Why all the secrecy? Why doesn't Jesus simply come out and say who he is and what he is about? In modern lingo, "Jesus, why don't you stop playing games?" Before we venture to address our questions, perhaps Jesus would want to ask us one, namely, "Who is really playing games, me or you?" In other words, is our bewilderment and impatience over this secrecy a genuine desire to have Jesus proclaimed or is it just a symptom of our life today? We live in an age which is very protective of its right to know. Every secret is really a cover-up. And our right to know covers every conceivable aspect of life. Never mind *why* we want to know or what benefit to self or others information serves; to be in the know is its own reward. The proliferation of talk shows, TV News magazines, Hollywood gossip books, autobiographies of the great and near great, not to mention the countless number of weekly "shock sheets," testify to our craving for secret knowledge. We are fast becoming a generation of "new gnostics" in which the secrets of the powerful and famous cannot wait for the end time; secrets must be shouted from the roof tops today! When someone cures the sick and raises the dead we must know all there is to know.

Let us now return to our original question: Why is Jesus so secretive about being the Messiah? Jesus' secrecy comes from his fear of being misunderstood. Every epoch has its superstars and heroes(ines). Many times, the gospels tell us the people want to carry Jesus off and make him their king. Many want to manipulate and use Jesus for their own selfish ends. The Zealots want to politicalize Jesus in an effort to unite the people and throw the hated Romans out. More troubling than the political and military aspirations of some is the misunderstanding associated with the healing ministry of Jesus. There is a

danger that the cures of Jesus will be interpreted as the elimination of all suffering and
hardship. Jesus as the Messiah is going to rescue
us from trials and the limitations of the human
condition. However, we cannot paint Jesus as a
"Magic Messiah" who takes away all our problems in an instant. We cannot do this anymore
than we can paint Jesus as a modern revolutionary or political freedom fighter. Jesus as the
Messiah must suffer, be rejected, and *then* rise
to life with the Father. Jesus is the Messiah come
to liberate humankind from its true enemies: sin
and death. Jesus' destiny is interwoven with the
cross. The disciple can only be in communion
with Jesus to the extent that he partakes of the
cross and its sufferings.

In our more cynical moments maybe we could
view the Messianic secrecy as a game. Maybe
Jesus is the master psychiatrist and is using
reverse psychology. For every time Jesus warns
the cured to "zip their lip" they can't wait to
spill the beans. The more Jesus tells them to be
silent the more they proclaim what Jesus has
done. Maybe that was Jesus' intent all along: the
more he tells people to be silent the more they
will speak. However, this is too cynical. I prefer
to believe that what we see taking place is the
"gospel dynamic". That is, the gospel is "good
news" and such news, God's love and care, is
too good to keep to one's self. Sheer joy spills

over in a public proclamation of what God has done for his people through Jesus. Such a dynamic is important for us. What has God done for us lately? Have we been filled with gospel joy? Perhaps Jesus as Messiah is still the best kept secret we have. No one will ever know Jesus is Lord by looking at us. No sir. We won't spill the beans. Jesus' secret is safe with us. Oh well, poor Jesus, sometimes even the Messiah can't win!

Getting Stoned

IF one is expecting to find Jesus' views on drugs in what follows, I am afraid you will be disappointed. The gospels tell us that often the crowd was upset and confused by what Jesus said and did. Their anger was not limited to words; on several occasions they sought to get their hands on him. Perhaps the ugliest incident takes place when the crowd picks up stones to throw at Jesus (Jn. 10:25-39). He manages to escape without injury. This incident, and others that reflect crowd violence, indicate that Jesus not only had difficulty with his identity, but also with his conduct or actions.

We who are some 2,000 years removed from this episode no doubt want to ask: Why does the crowd want to stone Jesus? Jesus seems to be presenting the thesis that it is because he does good works. This, however, makes little sense. The crowd is quick to tell Jesus just that: "It is not for any good deed that we are stoning you." The people want to stone Jesus for claiming to be God's Son. Jesus is a blasphemer. In effect, Jesus is getting his not for his doing, but for who he claims to be. Jesus is just a stone's throw away from a good deal of pain because the crowd does not perceive the harmony between being and doing. Maybe this is another reason why Jesus was so reluctant to let the "Messianic Secret" out. It is easy for us to blame the crowd and, in the contemporary phrase, "lay a guilt trip" on them. The crowd is spiritually blind and they refuse to see the Sonship of Jesus. However, this seems "too heavy" an interpretation. The defect in the crowd is not so much theological as it is sociological. Jesus is being understood as another "do-gooder" and the people resent it. The crowd wants to be beholden to no one— Messiah or carpenter notwithstanding. Is their reaction really so strange? Not if we examine our experience and our feelings toward the "good works" of others.

Often we give to others of our time, energy, talents, and devotion. We become very good at giving without limits and never counting the cost or looking for a reward. Perhaps too good. In the midst of all our doing good some ingrate steps up and says, "But I don't want your help. Please mind your business." We are left in a state of shock and deeply hurt. We impulsively want to grab the barbarian and say, "Don't you see all that I am doing for you? Don't you see all I am saving you from? How could you say such a thing to me?" In other words, we would be asking, "Why have you stoned me with your words? Why have you bruised me with your ingrati-

tude? Which of my good works do you find offensive?" We would be in the same situation as
Jesus. Our doing good is not being perceived to
be in harmony with our claims of who we are:
friend, helper, and lover. No doubt we would
want to say the fault lies in the other person's in-
gratitude or blindness. We are being misunderstood and not seen in the right light.

But is this really the case? Perhaps our doing
and being for others is all too revealing. At times
our doing good can be a subtle manipulation, an
effort to possess and control the other. At times
we want the other to be so much in our debt that
they can never "pay us back". The other remains forever in our debt and we are only too
glad to remind them of this. Doing good for
others can become a sinister form of power. We
do for others so that we can become indispens-
able in their lives. We become the one whom
others cannot do without. Is it any wonder that
so much doing good or charity has fallen into ill
repute? Such hostility is expressed not only on
the interpersonal level, but also among nations.
How often do those countries who receive our
foreign aid (charity) show contempt rather than
gratitude? Maybe our help is being perceived as
an attempt to manipulate and control.

Does all of this mean we should stop being
charitable and doing good for others? Of course
not. It does mean we need to examine our

motives and take seriously our ability to deceive ourselves and others. There are no pure and absolutely good intentions in a fallen world. Our doing good does give us a feeling of power and control. The rather abrupt words of Jesus when someone called him good serve as a useful reminder: "Why do you call me good? There is only one who is good, your Father in heaven." Even in our doing good we need to pray for forgiveness and ask for God's cleansing grace. We are still unworthy servants just doing what is required. Furthermore, Jesus serves as the model for all our doing good. Jesus does not want to be a solution to all our problems in a magical way. Jesus will not be our king who has the power to grant our every whim and want. Jesus rejects this because he comes to enable people to hear, see, walk, experience liberty and life for themselves. Jesus is the one who ministers to people's needs, not wants. The miracles and good works of Jesus always point to a deeper reality: the loving presence of God the Father. Jesus never uses his service to insure his being served.

The ministry of Jesus is important for our daily Christian life with its great emphasis on service and fraternal charity. Our task is not so much to produce as to empower, free, and enhance the lives of those *with* whom we work. The good works we perform should always have this end: liberate others to do and be for themselves and others. Charity and love are signs of freedom and respect for the human person. We can never allow the other to become our permanent project and personal "ego trip". The next time we do for others and they want to make us king or queen, remember the stones as well as the crown. Cries of hosannah have a strange way of becoming "crucify him . . . crucify him".

Healing

THE human attractiveness of Jesus and the power of his divinity come together on the subject of healing. The God-Man Jesus is sensitive to the needs of others: their hunger, pain, spiritual dryness, and being lost. The people need healing and Jesus is the Divine Physician and Good Shepherd who restores them to health. We need to ask: What is the motivation for Jesus' healing others? Why is Jesus the authentic healer? And what does healing have to do with the Christian life today?

The motivation for the healing ministry of Jesus is compassion. That seems simple and innocent enough. Yet, there is a danger lurking. The root meaning of compassion is "to stoop down". Compassion is associated with a condescending or patronizing form of behavior. Too often this is the case. Our compassion often slips into a giving or doing for others out of our *superiority* rather than out of our common human vulnerability. Yet scripture clearly states, "Jesus had compassion." Jesus "stooped down" to suffering humanity out of selfless love (*agape*). Such a love seeks no reward. What could the lame, blind, possessed, and hungry give Jesus? Nothing. Nothing but their humanity which enriched the humanity of Jesus. In Jesus, God stoops down to man graciously, that is, in the spirit of grace. God can meet our needs, and we have the courage to accept God's initiative, because God became one like us in Jesus. Jesus is God's word that he is *for us*. Jesus is the neediness of God meeting the neediness of man.

Jesus is the authentic healer because healing means *wholeness*. The compassion of Jesus moves beyond the physical and material to include the spirit. Jesus does not ignore or disvalue the physical needs of people; quite the contrary, Jesus is sensitive to hunger and pain. But Jesus goes further and seeks to lead the one being healed to experience God directly at work in the human condition. Miracles of healing are signs which point to a deeper reality—God's love which brings wholeness to our fragmented condition. If the lame only walk, the blind receive only physical sight, the mute speak only human language, and the hungry are fed that which perishes, then Jesus is not the Divine Healer but the Divine Deceiver. The healing by Jesus is authentic because it goes to the depth of the one in need. Real healing touches the consciousness in which one listens to God in Holy Silence.

The ministry of healing does not end with Jesus, but it continues throughout history. Healing is central to the ministry of the Church and

the individual Christian. The healing presence of
the Crucified and Risen Lord remains active in
various ways: the sacraments, the quality of interpersonal relationships, and of course through
the Church. The Church, as the *gathering* people
of God, serves as the locus, sign, and event of
healing. The healing ministry of the Church is
especially revealed in its sacramental ministry
of reconciliation and the Eucharist. The Church
continues to announce the forgiving and accepting word of God to those who are alienated and
in the grip of sin and guilt. Not only is God's
word announced, it is proclaimed through the
community's actively seeking out those who
have "traveled to a distant land". The Church is
the forgiving Father who is always overcome
with joy at the son and daughter who come
home. The People of God always rejoice with the
good news that the one who was lost is now
found; the one who was thought to be dead has
now come back to life. Reconciliation calls for
celebration, that is, it calls for a banquet of
thanksgiving—the Eucharist.

The healing ministry of the Church which
begins with reconciliation is *completed* in the
Eucharist. One of the most touching scenes in all
of Scripture is reported in the thirteenth chapter
of St. John's Gospel. After Jesus washes the
disciple's feet and explains its meaning, he

reclines once more with them. Jesus tells the disciples one of them is going to betray him. The disciples are concerned to find out who is the one. Jesus says it is the one who receives the piece of bread dipped in the dish. Jesus gives the morsel to Judas. Is there any deeper meaning here than the indication that Judas is the traitor? Yes. According to the religious and cultural mores, the one who receives the first morsel is most honored, loved, and held in high regard. The first morsel is a sign of affection, tenderness, and the need for reconciliation. The Fourth Gospel paints Jesus as extending the peace of God to Judas. Jesus loves them *all* to the end. He loves not only the good, strong, and faithful. Jesus loves the weak in faith; those who deny him; and even those who betray him. Jesus is love incarnate and everything Jesus does is for one purpose: to reveal the very nature of God— suffering, reconciling love.

When we gather to celebrate the Eucharist we remember the Lord and live in hope until he comes again. And until he comes we are incomplete, restless, and fragmented. We too are in need of healing and reconciliation. The Christian community is not above the healing it ministers and the words of forgiveness are for the Church as well. Healing is not magic, but a sign of God's presence in our life at the point of

our physical and spiritual needs. Healing is a
sign that God is *for* us. The One who lives in unapproachable mystery has "stooped down" to
us in the form of a child and the Man of Sorrows.
It is our vocation to heal one another.

Forgiving and Forgetting

OUR vocabularies often become cluttered with what might be termed "buzz words". "Buzz words" are those often-used expressions that make the rounds at seminars, public lectures, and workshops. "Buzz words" are magical little words or phrases that prove one is in the know and up on the latest movement or wave of the future. "Buzz words" catch our attention, but often cover over the complexity of the issue under discussion. Examples of "buzz words" are "sensitivity," "dialogue," "get in touch with one's feelings," "being open," "broaden your horizon," and "community," to name but a few. Forgiveness has become one of the "buzz words" that so often makes the homily rounds. "When in doubt, preach about forgiveness" is a cardinal rule of Homiletics 101. Forgiveness is a safe topic. You can't go wrong speaking about forgiveness. No sir. The bishop will be happy and the congregation won't hold back their contributions. No feathers are ruffled. Forgiveness is so neat and clean. Such a view is true, to a point. As long as forgiveness is *talked* about, *homilized* about, and *intellectualized* about, forgiveness is safe. However, should forgiveness spill over into our everyday lives, then feathers are ruffled and things become rather messy. Anyone who has given forgiveness a try learns how dangerous it can be. Yet, anyone who is serious about the Gospel knows how essential forgiveness is.

The real stumbling block to authentic forgiveness is our inability to *forget*. If in our forgiving we can still keep an account of the injuries and offenses done to us, then forgiveness isn't so tough. If we don't have to pay the price of letting go of the past we can forgive. But if we must both forgive and forget, well, that is too much to ask. Our attitude toward forgiveness is often like the dog who buries a bone, but never forgets where the bone is buried. At the right time the bone can be resurrected. So it is with us. At the appropriate time we too can dig up the past so as to fill our present with anger and destroy future reconciliation. The words of the prophet Jeremiah can be of great importance, "I (Yahweh) will forgive them and remember their sins no more" (Jer. 31:34ff). Not only does Yahweh forgive, but he also forgets.

A few years ago the conventional wisdom assured us that "love means you never have to say you're sorry". Experience teaches us how shallow this is. In the web of relationships that structure our everyday (family, parish, school, business, clubs) we realize how necessary it is to forgive and be forgiven. Forgiveness by itself is insufficient to rebuild relationships. Forgiving demands forgetting and nothing less is sufficient for today's Church. Our forgiveness cannot be as dry as the proverbial dust. Forgiveness demands we extend the kiss of peace, anoint with the oil of gladness, and baptize the worth of the other. Only then will our words and actions be more than duty or sacramental function. Real forgiveness produces healing at the very core of one's being. Forgiveness liberates the person to realize his or her best possibilities. The grip of past guilt is broken. Genuine forgiveness opens the future so we can live in hope and freedom. To forgive and accept forgiveness is essential to our nature as one who is made in God's image and called to grow in the Divine likeness.

Father Henri Nouwen tells the following story: There once was an old man who used to meditate each morning on the bank of the river. One morning after meditation he saw a scorpion floating helplessly in the water. The scorpion was struggling to climb onto a stump that lined the banks of the river. The old man reached out his hand to rescue the scorpion. As soon as he touched it, the scorpion stung him. The old man pulled back his hand. Again and again the old man tried to rescue the scorpion, and each time he was stung. His hand had become a swollen, bloody mess. A passerby saw this and shouted to the old man, "Hey, stupid old man, why are you doing that for an ungrateful creature that will only sting you and cause you pain?" The old man replied, "Because it is in the nature of the scorpion to sting, why should I give up my own nature which is to save?" Why indeed?

Genuine Christian forgiveness demands a convenient memory, that is, a memory that knows when and what to forget. The greatest obstacle to forgiveness and reconciliation is fear. Fear of rejection; of being misunderstood; of being seen as meek, which is too often equated with being weak—all are stumbling blocks to healing and growth. There is a great potential in each of us to love and heal. What is needed is the courage to allow God's forgiving Spirit to work in our hearts and dispel the emotional fear that keeps us timid. The next time a two-legged scorpion comes along and stings us, how shall we respond?

Is That All There Is?

ACCORDING to folklore and story-telling, which often makes religion so attractive and human, St. John liked to address his community with these words: "Little children, love one another. Little children, love one another." One day a "radical theologian" challenged John by saying, "All you ever say is love one another. That message is so familiar as to be tiring. It is threadbare by now. Don't you have any new insights?" No doubt our radical theologian felt that John would benefit from a summer seminar or a crash course in homiletics. But with great patience John responded, "There is no more profound insight into the person of Jesus and eternal life than for the members of the community to love one another." Such a simple and powerful answer. However, if John was challenged in his own day, one can only imagine what would happen to him in the "secular city" of today in a world "come of age". John would be labeled an official curia theologian. His writings would find no publisher. He probably couldn't get a teaching position. No doubt students would complain, "We know all that. I am so bored because you're so boring!" A theology department chairperson could only shudder at the results of that most infallible of teacher performance indicators: the student evaluation form. Poor John would certainly flounder in obscurity.

It will profit us to ask if we are missing the insight for which John has been so identified, namely, love? What is John really telling us about love and its application to human life and community?

The old message of love is really a new message for two important reasons. First, man did not know how to truly love until out of love God sent his only Son to redeem the world. Before Jesus love was narrow, finite, and self-serving. Love was extended to one's family, countrymen, or some finite possession or honor. But with the coming of Jesus and the Cross, we glimpse what real love entails: universality, sacrifice, and suffering. Love reaches out to all who are in need regardless of status or merit. Christian love demands a willingness to love ultimately, that is, one must be ever ready to lay down one's life for the other. Christian love is not "pie in the sky" or pietistic idealism. Just the opposite is the case. Christian love is hard realism and demands courage. The story recorded in the Fourth Gospel between Jesus and the woman caught in adultery (Jn. 8) best exemplifies the hard realism of Christ-like love and acceptance. The confrontation between Jesus and the woman is very disappointing to the modern mind. Jesus does not excuse her adultery because of a genetic condition, socio-economic factors, or a rather unfortunate zodiac pattern. Jesus makes it clear: she is an adultress. She is guilty, and no amount of rationalization is going to change that. Perhaps this seems lacking in pastoral sensitivity. However, Jesus does that which is essential to love, healing, and growth. Jesus *accepts* her as guilty. He accepts her as she is: an adultress. *Then* he challenges her to live in an authentic way. Jesus pays her the highest compliment by taking her situation seriously. Her sin and guilt are recognized, but they are not all-determining and destructive. The real issue is not her adultery by itself, but rather, the real issue is the woman as a child of God being challenged to live in a new way. Jesus penetrates the exterior, sees her heart, and extends God's love. Love becomes incarnate in Jesus and the woman. There is no love *in general*. Love is particular and localized in the human and situational elements.

Secondly, this message ever old and ever new is always relevant because, as humans who live "East of Eden," we forget, sin, and fall short of our potentials and the glory of God. We need to be constantly reminded of our vocation to love as God first loved us. Perhaps our impatience with "love-talk" comes from the realization that there is so little real love behind all the talk of love. Love does not float in the Platonic world of ideas. Love is found in the social marketplace of daily life. Love is found in doing one's duty; cleaning the house; caring for children; being a good provider on a material and spiritual level; and daily committing oneself to do what is required. The Christian love ethic demands our best. As G. K. Chesterton so wisely said: Christianity has not been tried and found wanting. Christianity has been tried and found too hard!

To accept the invitation of Jesus, "Follow Me ... Come and see," means that one also makes a commitment to live in community or church. There is no such thing as individualized Christianity, if by that one means we go it alone. The community dimension of Christianity goes against the American grain or ethos. We value our privacy which has become an almost absolute right. In fact, privacy is the basis for the Supreme Court's abortion decision. The mother's right to privacy is greater than the unborn child's right to live. In addition, we Americans are rugged individualists who often view interpersonal relationships as entanglements to our freedom. We handle work better than we manage our one-to-one associations. The American hero is a loner and ahistoric. He has no past. He mysteriously appears on the scene we know not where from. He is unattached, with no children, wife, or friends. The American hero simply *is*. He often must encounter evil or some injustice to right and then leaves, moving on to the next challenge. The American hero has no roots and he cannot be tied down. He is a wanderer. The classical American hero is, of course, *Shane*.

So much of modern life has one thing in common with *Shane* and other heroes: loneliness and the search for community. The young are often driven to religious cults not because they are bad or shallow, but because they are good and idealistic. They are looking for something to believe in and sacrifice for. They want to belong and be recognized and valued as a human being with a name. The Christian experience and symbol system have much to offer our fellow seekers. Within our tradition that which is being sought is there for the taking. Love, sacrifice, discipline, hope, and community are the non-negotiables of our rich tradition. The present crises of loneliness and alienation often result from our forgetting what is most attractive and enduring in our heritage. But don't worry. Jesus knew this all along. To keep us in the truth he gave us the Paraclete. The God who is with us and for us is also within us.

PART III
God within Us

When Bio-Rhythms Are Low

THE "stories" told so far have have centered on God with us and God for us. God is not only our loving Father and Creator; God is also our redeemer and at work in Jesus. Jesus is God's Word of love who heals us of alienation and estrangement. However, our story is not complete, for the best is yet to be. Our God, who revealed himself in Jesus, is Lord and alive! Our God lives deep within each of us through the active presence of the Spirit. The life and death of Jesus is more than a beautiful story filled with ideals and nobility. The empty tomb is not the end, but signals the beginning of God within us. Jesus is not a model in the sense of someone whom we can imitate, but who always remains external to us. For example, one can be a devoted Socratic philosopher but never experience Socrates as alive. Through the gift of the Holy Spirit, Jesus is alive within us and challenging us to growth through responsible freedom. The story of God's love within us was not easy to come by. It was certainly not easy for those first disciples after the shattering experience of that anything but Good Friday.

We are indebted to St. Luke for his account of

the two disciples on the road to Emmaus (Lk. 24: 13-35). How can we describe the disciples? Without a moment's hesitation we would say: their bio-rhythms were quite low. Physically, emotionally, spirtually, and mentally they were like the Dow-Jones reacting to bad news—down. They were men without hope, vision, or meaning. They were very much absorbed in their own concerns, disappointments, and feelings of being betrayed. Without too much exaggeration we could say these disciples were suffering from the "me syndrome". The disciples expected so much from Jesus and got so little in return. They left everything for this religious guru and lost it all. Their families, reputations, comfortable way of life were gone; a thing of the past. How can we explain their "irrational" attraction to this itinerant preacher? No doubt they were "brain-washed" by Jesus. They became a mindless cult. They wouldn't have followed him if he hadn't put a spell over them. Maybe it was something in the fish or the loaves. However he did it, Jesus brainwashed them—no doubt about it. With the tragic and disillusioning "end" of Jesus still fresh in their minds they resolved never to give in to blind faith again. No more disillusionment. Only tough realism from now on. They will believe the words and signs of no one anymore.

And yet, something happens to these converted realists. They encounter a stranger who

Maestri

isn't up on the latest gossip, or hasn't read the latest issue of the *Jewish Inquirer*. The disciples fill the Stranger in on the stubborn and ineludible facts of the case. Jesus was a great prophet in word and deed. The authority structure put him to death. With that the hope of freedom came crashing down. Some women found an empty tomb and had a vision of angels who say Jesus is alive. However, this is probably just hysteria. In the process of telling the story a transformation begins to take place. The Stranger in their midst fills them with an inner burning, with light and nourishment. The Stranger becomes a stranger no longer, in fact, he seems all too familiar. Could it be? Perhaps the women were right? Wait. We've been through this before. More will be required this time. Remember the disciples are now tough realists.

If more is required so be it. More will be given. This Stranger nourishes them through word and sacrament; book and table. The Stranger gives them a crash course in Scripture. The disciples are grateful so they want the Stranger to stay with them. The mask of the Stranger is now completely removed: they share a meal and their eyes are opened. The Stranger is now exposed: it is Jesus and he is alive. The bad news has become good news. Their hearts are burning and they must proclaim this story. It should be noted that the disciples come to experience Jesus in the context of sharing a meal. There is nothing more ordinary and necessary than eating. It is in this everyday ritual that the disciples experience Jesus as still with, for, and within them. The meal becomes a sacrament, that is, a revelation of the holy in the midst of the profane. The call to newness of life, the struggle of discipleship, and the encounter with the Risen Lord are found within the demands of ordinary, everyday life. The Risen Lord is not found in the spectacular or flashy. Jesus is within and among us. The disciples have their eyes opened to the active presence of God, and this is the good news. What God has done in Jesus is not *information*, but news. And news this good must be proclaimed. It cannot be kept to one's self. It is a news that demands a telling and a living.

What do the disciples on the road to Emmaus have to say to us? They want to say that we too travel that same road. There is a little of the Emmaus experience in our own hearts. Life takes its toll on each of us. We too are at times without hope, sight, resolve, and faith. We too are caught in the iron jaws of doubt. We question and wonder. We give up so much; hope so much; expect so much; and at times seem to get so little in return. The flame in our hearts grows cold. Our bio-rhythms run low from time to time. We need someone to rouse and renew us. The

Church continues to call the Disciples of Emmaus to book and table, word and sacrament. The task of the Church is to continue to inflame hearts, open Scripture, and invite people to "stay with us". The drama of Emmaus is the drama of the Church. But that Stranger? We too must ask: Who is he? We must experience the answer for ourselves. Do you think he lives within us too? Pray for the courage to say, "Lord stay with us. Lord stay with me."

Growth

IN the previous section (God for Us) we spoke of
Jesus calling the community and the individual
Christian to express love for one another as he
loved them. Such love is the distinguishing mark
of the disciple of Christ. The need for growth
and the enrichment of the quality of our interpersonal relationships are a constant Christian challenge. At first blush this challenge
seems quite easy. In any drugstore or book outlet
one can find dozens of books devoted to the
development of personality and the cultivation
of friends. "How-to" books are filled with the
new gnosticism offering us the secret knowledge
of winning friends and influencing people.
However, the books of Holy Scripture want to
suggest a different image and source: the im-
agery of the vine and the source of the Holy
Spirit.

We all know it takes a great deal of care and
patience to allow something to grow. With
flowers, vines, and certainly people, we have to
pay attention to individual makeups and needs.
Many of the sensitivities employed in the growth
of nature apply to the human person as well.
Some people need help to adapt to hostile en-

vironments without losing their luster. Some must be sheltered while others need exposure to the harsher realities of life for their own good. Still others need "space" so as to grow at their own pace and inner dynamic. Sensitivity is needed if one is to read the cues or signals given off by others; especially in moments of silence and restlessness. We must hear what is being said and, more importantly, what is *not* being said. All growth does not go smoothly. There is a need for maturity in reminding ourselves and others that patience is crucial for healing the hurts and falls of life. At times we need to give people the truth which prunes away the rough edges and weeds that can choke growth and life. If we are disciplined and sensitive enough we will be blessed with a rich harvest of friends; sturdy, graceful, creative, and ready to bear fruit. However, we cannot do it alone. Growth in interpersonal relationships ultimately involves grace and the work of the Holy Spirit.

The image of the vine is beautifully expressed in the Fourth Gospel (Ch. 15). Israel is initially viewed as a vine planted by Yahweh. Israel, the vine of Yahweh, is brought out of slavery in Egypt into the Promised Land of freedom (Ps. 80). But now the true vine, Jesus, has come to liberate humankind from sin and death, and free us to love. It is only through our continued abiding in Jesus and he within us that we have the hope of growing into the full measure of Christian adulthood. Apart from Jesus we cannot really love and accept love. All of our efforts, achievements, and successes are shallow if done apart from Christ. Our love is selfish and possessive. There is no magic cure or technique in any how-to book that can liberate us to be truly for the other as much as we are for ourselves. Such liberation only comes through grace and the abiding presence of the Spirit within us. The Spirit does not merely change our external behavior, but the Spirit inwardly liberates us to realize our best possibilities.

Many of the contemporary how-to books promise instant results and success. The work of the Spirit within us promises no such magic. The conversion of the heart, from stone to flesh, takes patience, struggle, and growth. It is a lifelong process. Some theologians even go so far as to hypothesize an after-life of spiritual maturation in which one continues to grow into the likeness of God, or what St. Irenaeus called "soul-making". There are, in effect, worlds within worlds of growth that extend beyond the limits of earthly space and time. What theologians are saying is that patience and perserverance are essential to authentic growth. Such growth is only possible through the transforming work of the Spirit.

A life centered on Christ, animated by the

Spirit, calls for openness and courage on our part. To be a Christian is to commit oneself to adventure. There is no playing it safe or "cool". Jesus often reserves his harshest criticisms for those who refuse to grow and bury their talents. The opposite of Christian existence and love is fear. Fear is an existential decision in which, through our freedom, we refuse to grow, risk, and trust. We freely refuse to make a leap of faith. Instead we seek our security in the world of things and the work of our own hands. We build idols of sex, power, money, and reputation. The invitation to "Follow Me . . . Come and see" is rejected as absurd and foolish. The decision to leave all and follow Jesus is a difficult one indeed. Yet, all growth is painful. We grow as we seek to respond to the challenge of the Spirit. This is not all bad. Pain is a sign we are alive and aware of some basic reorientation of our values and life-style. Only the dead experience no pain.

Perhaps the most painful aspect of growth is the need to *change*. We must pour out the old wine and grow new skin. Change has become a "fear word" in our society. In fact, Alvin Toffler has powerfully presented the case for "future shock". It is not only the quantity of change that has so overwhelmed us, but it is the *rate* of change which causes such great disorientation. Adaptation on a social and individual level demands a sufficient time-lag. This "time be-tween" allows continuity and order in the various stages of change. But the tremendous application of technology has eliminated, almost completely, the time lag between successive changes. Therefore, to speak about change often evokes in us a negative reaction. Not only is our aversion to change sociological, but it is theological as well. Sin is that force or power which clouds the future and undermines hope. We retreat into a seemingly secure past or present. We defend with all our might that which is, rather than that which could be, and by God's grace will be. Jesus knew how much change and the future can evoke fear in us. Jesus himself experienced this fear when "the hour of the cup" came to him. The Father sent an angel to strengthen him. In our own struggle with fear and change, Jesus sends us the Paraclete, the Holy Spirit to be active within us. We can change. We must change. And we can do so with confidence knowing and believing that the Spirit guides us and is even with us.

Peace at Any Price

WE spoke about the need for change and the fear that change evokes in us: fear of the unknown, of being misunderstood, of giving up the tried and secure, of being changed. And most of all, change evokes in us the fear of dying and the mystery of death. All of our energies and efforts, achievements and life's work are subject to the law of temporality and change. The world does pass away and we with it. We and all creation are in a state of "perpetual perishing". It is no wonder that change, the new, often taps the fears we work so hard to hide or deny. In the words of Dostoevsky: "taking a new step, uttering a new word, is what people fear most." It is so much easier for ourselves and others if we just "roll with the flow". There is no real need to disturb the waters. After all, isn't life too short? Why get all excited about that which seems so trivial in the long run? Isn't it our duty to live in peace with others? All of these questions, which in reality are assertions, are put forward in defense of the *status quo*. Such questions serve as an apologetic or rationalization for our love of comfortable advice. In time we come to view our feeling of comfort with the given order as a gift of tranquility and peace. We make peace with the world. We are *in* the world and we have now become *of* the world. We are at home. Yet, at the outset we must ask: can we, a pilgrim people, find our rest so easily? Maybe to ask such a question is reserved only for religious types and malcontents who are jealous of not being able to make peace with modernity. That *must* be it.

Ours is an age which seeks to live and let live. Every moral issue is settled by the categorical imperative which states, "as long as nobody else gets hurt, I am free to act as I determine." We are encouraged to "win friends and influence people." At all costs, we try never to offend, challenge, or upset the *status quo*. We must dialogue and be open to all things new. Our horizons must be expanded. We must be an offense to no one. We must learn the latest interpersonal techniques for friendship. Never bring up the wrong topics at parties: religion, politics, and ethical issues. After all, differences are just a matter of style, taste, or etiquette. There is no need to get all hot and bothered. If this code of behavior is violated a rather tragic fate awaits the modern Prometheus: banishment from all parties; career promotions come to an abrupt halt; and one is labeled controversial, revolutionary, or a religious fanatic. Your social world will be greatly limited. You will be forced to become your own best friend.

In a deeper way such a fate awaits the person of faith who seeks to walk in newness of life guided by the Spirit. The person of faith is a disturber of the peace and brings the sword of questioning and inquiry. The person of faith is a sign of contradiction to the conventional wisdom of the age. He-she is a challenger, a reproach, and an accusation against the well-worn values and taken-for-granted world. The person of faith is a living transvaluation of values in which those who weep now rejoice; those who are full go empty; the weak are made strong; and the last are now first. It is uncomfortable to have such people around. They evoke in us deep feelings that we would just as soon forget: restlessness that signals the need for change; incompleteness; existential dishonesty; anger and hostility; guilt. The world (in the Johannine sense of those powers which are under the influence of Satan) often responds to the person of faith with violence and ultimately death. Socrates had to drink the hemlock. Soren Kierkegaard had to drink from the bitter cup of ridicule. Jesus brought the world the last thing it wanted to hear: the good news of forgiveness and God's love. Humankind prefers the darkness and the shadow world of illusion. Especially if such illusions can serve to rationalize the living of each day for ourselves alone. The good news of Jesus is bad news for those who wish to blame their behavior or attitude on an uncaring or absent God. The response of the world to those who challenge, question, and offer new possibilities is a sorry and tragic one of hemlock, ridicule, and the cross.

The gift of peace and the inner feeling of wholeness does not come at a cheap price. Those who dream dreams and see visions must be prepared to pay a price; sometimes the ultimate price. T. S. Eliot once remarked, "Humankind cannot bear very much reality." Too much light causes blindness and a feeling of at-homeness in the darkness that covers so much of our contemporary history. Peace calls for courage the way Aristotle understood courage: the willingness to suffer in the short-term in order to achieve some long-term good. One must even be willing to deny some immediate good for a greater good. Courage calls for wisdom and the ability to see through the apparent goods or idols which try to control us. All of this is saying that peace cannot be sentimentalized or handed over to pious thoughts. Peace demands tough realism. The New Eon ushered in through the birth of Jesus is still a hope. Nations have not beaten their swords into plowshares and spears into pruning forks. Nations still train for war and hide their anxiety behind a mask of strong words. Our so-called balance of power, as an insurance of peace, is in reality a balance of terror. On the interpersonal level our words to each other still express anger, deception, and game-playing. Our world still believes that might makes right and meekness is weakness. We still search for the peace which quiets our desperation in the GNP or mighty weapons of destruction. The world still has difficulty looking to the Crib and the Cross for peace and hope. In the Child and the Crucified One there is so little power, so little resources, and so little apparent might. There is *only* the power of suffering, enduring love. So, we continue to place our hopes for peace in the glory of man's wisdom which is folly to God, and to forget the wisdom of God which is foolishness to our age.

The work and hope of peace lies with the Christian in the marketplace. Our confidence and hope for peace are not based on our efforts alone. Humanistic sentiment is necessary but never sufficient. All humanism is in need of redemption, that is, is in need of Jesus and the work of the Spirit. It is the Spirit who gives us the courage and vision to replace old myths with new possibilities. The Spirit enables us to venture forth into the unknown trusting the light of faith to guide the way. The Spirit works *within and through* our human freedom. The Spirit does not replace the need for good judgment and hard work. As moral philosopher David McGuire says, "grace favors the well prepared mind."

The Christian community looks to the One who said Yes to our condition, and handed over the Spirit to that community in history which continues to endure all, believe all, and hope all. Oh yes—hopes all. The community that is hopefully confident enough to sing, "Let there be peace on earth and let it begin with me."

Those Last Things

IN our discussion of change and the fear that change evokes, especially the fear of death, we must be careful not to trivialize such feelings. It is built into our condition to want to cling to the safe and familiar. If there has been an essential shift in the contemporary mind it is this: an acute awareness of process, evolution, and the temporality of all that is. To live in the modern world is to be aware of the historical conditioning of all reality. In being historically sensitive we become increasingly sensitive about death. Our initial response is natural enough—denial. We cover over death by placing it in an indefinite future or apply death to others in a general way but never to us. We say, "Everyone must die someday." Also, "Death comes for everybody." It is only when we say, "Death will come *for me*, and it may be *today*," that the existential power of death is most felt. The funeral industry does its best to shield the family from grief. We often hear it said, "He looks better now than when he was alive." Psychiatrist Erich Fromm is of the opinion that the wake is the last social event one must endure. We do not speak about death, rather we say someone has "passed away" or is "no longer with us". Religion itself can serve as an escape from facing the reality of death. We try to short circuit the grieving process by appeals to pious sentiments: "Don't cry, mother's in heaven now." But grief needs to be expressed and honored as a truly human response to this evil. Jesus wept at the death of Lazarus, all the while speaking of the hope of resurrection. Religion ought not to be used to repress what is most expressive of our condition. Death has replaced sex as the taboo subject. At all cost we keep the young from learning about pain, suffering, and death. Death and sickness are isolated in hospitals. Death is the "too much of reality" which we cannot stand. The unfortunate consequence of this denial of death is that, not only do we fail to understand death and its meaning, but we fail to understand the meaning of life. Our life only makes sense because there is an end-time; a finality. To confront death while living is to be on the road to authentic existence.

The thought naturally arises: Fine, we learn to accept our own finality and death. It is "me" who is going to die, and perhaps today. Does this not leave us with what might be termed a "resolution of despair"? In the final analysis I am going to die. Period. That's all there is. In the end there is no *ultimate* difference between the person who seeks to live honestly and for others, and the one who lives only for the self. Both share a common destiny. Therefore, isn't hope an illusion? These questions áre well taken. However, a respectful no seems in order. The Christian system calls us to hope, to be sure, and to seek eternal life and resurrection. But this is not an escape into some distant future. Resurrection and eternal life are *present* realities.

There is a branch of theology which deals with death, judgment, heaven, hell, and the end of the world. This theological speciality is called *eschatology*. The word itself means, "the last or end things". There are many types of eschatology. The writer of the Fourth Gospel develops his own eschatological perspective which Biblical scholars call "realized eschatology". What this means is that one does not have to wait for bodily death to be judged. Eternal life or condemnation is part of our everyday existence. Every day one is confronted with the decision of faith or disbelief. Every day is a trial and the jury is always in session weighing the evidence. Who is the jury that renders these daily verdicts? It is none other than we ourselves through the decisions we make and fail to make. Eternal life or condemnation are not in the distant, indefinite future, but realized in the here and now. St. John says, "he who hears my words and believes *has* eternal life." "He who loves the brethren *has already* passed from death to life." Such a perspective is important for three reasons. First, the present cannot be trivialized. We cannot take tomorrow for granted, or look to the past as an insurance policy for a future reward. Second, the everyday, ordinary life of the Christian takes on ultimate importance. Our final destiny is determined by the quality of our everydays in terms of charity and faith. Finally, judgment is not the result of God's anger or capricious will, but is the result of our free decisions. It is we who pass judgment on ourselves by the way we choose to live.

The Fourth Gospel speaks about eternal life and its present importance. The Synoptic gospels and the Pauline writings speak about our hope of resurrection. Concerning this hope two important points need to be mentioned: resurrection is not immortality, and secondly, resurrection is also a present reality. The Christian hope is not for immortality and the endless duration of earthly existence. The Christian hope is not even for a bodily existence of indefinite duration in another location such as heaven. Few of us would want to live endlessly in our present condition. We do not hope merely for days of life, but we hope for life to our days. The Christian resurrection hope is for a direct participation in the glorified and Spirit filled life of Jesus as Lord. We want to "know Christ and the power of His resurrection". The Christian hopes for human existence in its fullness, completeness, and wholeness. The Christian hopes for transformation, perfection, and liberation. We do not hope to become less human, but through Jesus and the power of the Spirit, we hope to realize our full potentials.

The hope of resurrection is not placed in the future at the traditionally classified end of the world. Resurrection is not the rather unbelievable spectacle of dead bodies popping up out of the ground. Resurrection is a process whereby we become less and less so Jesus through the Spirit becomes more and more. Resurrection is a process of decentralization whereby the selfish and pridefilled ego is transformed into the image of God revealed in Jesus. The importance of process cannot be overestimated. Resurrection is not magic or some quick fix for what ails us. Rather, resurrection is a life-long struggle to know God as our Father, Jesus as Brother, and the Spirit as the Giver of Gifts. In this process of "growing less" we really become fully alive. No longer do we live for ourselves, but it is now Christ living in us. The hope of resurrection is at work in our everyday lives helping us to see the world and ourselves anew. The Spirit alive in Jesus as Lord is calling us to this same newness of life.

All that has been said so far comes to a head at this juncture: the Christian is a person of hope and joy. Eternal life and resurrection are not futurist escapes or subject to a Marxian critique of pie in the sky. They are calls to take each day seriously by loving God and serving our neighbors. Such hopes as eternal life and resurrection do not leave us in a morbid, depressing state of affairs so common with much of existential literature. The Christian hope fills one with a joy the passing world cannot give and cannot take away. The Paraclete is God within us always whispering the good news of love. The Paraclete says to us, "look to the present, look to the now, for in the present the Eternal is breaking in and being revealed to the eye of faith." Pray God we have the courage to embrace that Reality!

Beware of Trojan Horses

IF there is one piece of ancient advice we have taken to heart it is this: beware of anyone who offers you a gift. The Trojan Horse is a fact of life and whenever one wants to give you something be careful, it's probably a trap. The specter of someone offering us a gift often signals a red alert and our defenses go into a state of maximum readiness. We can't help but feel that there is more to the gift than meets the eye. The ancient advice becomes contemporary wisdom: you can't get something for nothing, and you only get what you pay for. We need to ask what is it about gifts that causes so much discomfort, and secondly, what are the consequences for the Christian life and our understanding of God?

The American ethos has always placed great stock in experience as a teacher. And if experience teaches us anything it is that gifts often rob us of our freedom. When one accepts a gift at the same time one becomes beholden to the giver. No matter how freely the gift is given we often attach strings to it. We cannot help but wonder when and in what way will we have to pay for this gift. The giver of the gift will no

108

doubt feel he has a claim on our time or person. Our time is no longer our own. We must be on call to return the gift through some inconvenience to ourselves. After all, how can you say no to someone who gives you a gift? Maybe Sartre is right—hell is other people. They rob us of our freedom and lay claim to our agenda with a hidden one of their own. Perhaps it would be better to avoid all personal entanglements? That is, play it cool and "hang loose" when it comes to interpersonal relationships. At least your time is your own and your freedom is preserved.

Even if one is not concerned about freedom and a hidden agenda there are other problems with accepting gifts. We often associate the receiving of gifts with charity or welfare. Gifts have become associated with a handout and are often given to one who is needy or deficient. Charity has become associated with welfare and welfare is the worst of all social diseases. Welfare indicates one is lazy and nothing more than a legal rip-off artist. Welfare is an affront to our work ethic and the belief that one should work if one is to eat and make one's way in the world. Only for the most serious of reasons is one excused from working, and even then, the stigma of being on welfare is never completely removed. "Being on welfare" is to have a soiled identity which indicates one is not contributing to the daily efforts of life. In the long run, the very value and human worth of such a person is called into question. The identity of a welfare person is not an easy one to live with.

In addition to our being uncomfortable about the receiving of gifts, we are equally ill at ease about *giving* gifts. After all, what do we *have* that is worthy of our friend or loved one? What can we do or buy that is expressive of our deep feelings of love and respect? Where is the store that has just the right gift to say it all? Is there a book to be read that can give us the answer for the right gift to say just the right thing? Probably not. So we will continue to give our inadequate gifts and offer an apology all the while. "It isn't really much." "I wish I could have gotten you more." "If you don't like it you can always take it back." The litany that expresses our feelings of inadequacy is endless. Perhaps we have been asking the wrong question. Maybe it is not so much what we can do or buy, but who we can *be and become* that is at the heart of true gift giving. Ralph Waldo Emerson said it best: the authentic gift is one's self. It is not really what we do or buy, but the quality and sincerity of the giver. The fundamental gift in all giving is the offering of the personhood of the giver. Here is the real challenge and fear that comes with giving: every gift involves the self and often our self image is viewed as inadequate. When we apologize about the gift we give, we are often apologizing about our self. Our feelings of inadequacy, inferiority, and ungiftedness come to the surface. Every offering is filled with anxiety because implied in every gift is the placing of the self on the line. The self is that which is really offered with every gift. To reject or be less than enthusiastic about a gift is at the same time a statement of acceptance or rejection about the self. To accept my gift is to accept me and *vice versa*.

The difficulty we all experience with the giving and receiving of gifts has carryover in the Christian life. St. Paul and traditional Christian theology have understood the Holy Spirit as the Giver of Gifts. St. Paul in his Letter to the Corinthians speaks of the Spirit as the Giver of many gifts (I Cor. 12:4-11). However, doesn't this just compound our problem? For if we feel inadequate and defensive with our peers or loved ones, how much more so with God? What do we possibly have that God could use or desire? What could we possibly give God? Furthermore, isn't it God who rewards us for what we do and the good works we perform? God expects us to work, use our talents, and not expect a divine handout. Don't we say, "Pray but keep the gun powder dry"? Therefore, we have nothing God can use or want. And secondly, we are saved by our works and effort. These views are common and there is an element of truth in each of them.

However, that is what makes them so dangerous. They contain a partial truth, but the greater portion distorts our true relationship with God, the self, and others.

It is true enough that God does not need us in any essential sense of the word. God is not dependent for his Being on us. It is we who are dependent upon God as the Ground of our being. However, God does want to enter into relationship with each of us and the world. The Incarnation and the sending of the Spirit are testimonies of this. It is not that God wants something from us, but that God wants something *for* us. God wants us to live our life to the fullest and realize our best potential. God has a work, a vocation or aim, that is particular to each of us. This aim is God's gift or grace to help us realize our best and live life with zest. The Divine aim and lure is not a denial of our freedom. We are at liberty to deny the Divine aim and do our own thing. This is basically sin: the turning off of God in order to follow our own individualistic parade. The responsible use of freedom calls us to creatively respond to the Divine call in our given situation. There is no Divine blueprint or how-to book that relieves us of responsibility and of imaginatively responding to our world and its challenges. What God wants for us, and to give to us, is the opportunity to live life in his presence each day. His presence does not eliminate freedom or excuse us from the suffering of the cross. Discipleship has its cost. Does this mean that one must earn or work one's way to heaven? Is discipleship the hidden agenda and "Catch 22" of the divine gift?

Much of our experience, training, and values would want us to respond in the affirmative. Yes, we must prove to God that we are worthy of him by accomplishing a great deal. We need to impress God, and certainly others, by our faith, intellect, charity, and general religious behavior. It is only by doing all this that God will allow us into his company. However, the life of Jesus, the whole of Scripture, and the experience of the Christian community in its finer moments rejects this view. No one merits or earns heaven, if by such talk we mean that God owes us a place at his right and left hand. The good news of Jesus which is so hard for us to accept is the fact that we are accepted without condition. The Kingdom of God is within us and ours for the asking. The Scriptures testify that all that is done by God springs from a pure Divine Love without reservation. The creation of the world, the sending of the Son, and the giving of the Spirit are not and cannot be earned. We can only accept them in gratitude as a pure gift (grace) of love. This calls for us to exhibit a good deal of courage and the lowering of our defenses. Ultimately it means we must trust and be open to the Spirit. Such trusting openness causes us anxiety. We are so vulnerable and open to being hurt. It is only through the working of the Spirit that we have the courage and trust to say "Abba," that is, Father.

The Spirit, as God within us, calls us to realize our own giftedness. The Spirit liberates us to express our best selves and not fear rejection or hostility. Our gifts are not private possessions but community blessings to be used for the common good. The sharing of our gifts and talents with others does not lessen us, but enriches community life. Furthermore, we become enriched by receiving the gifts of others as an expression of love. The Christian community is the gathering and event of those who come in the Lord's name to receive and to give. The good God who spoke his ultimate Word in Jesus continues to say yes to each of us through the Spirit who dwells deep within.

Wisdom

THE gift of the Spirit by Jesus is a reminder of the faithfulness of God with us, for us, and within us. The Spirit is the active presence of God calling each of us to realize our own best possibilities. The Holy Spirit is not only a Giver of Gifts, but the Spirit is giftedness itself. The Scriptures and sacraments speak of the gifts of the Holy Spirit. These gifts of grace help to sustain us in the everyday struggles of Christian discipleship. Among the gifts of the Spirit none seems more crucial for us today than the gift of wisdom.

What has wisdom meant for humankind throughout history? Two great traditions help structure the Western conception of wisdom: the Greek and Hebrew. Those in ancient Greece who searched for wisdom had to travel the path that led to the oracle at Delphi. The message offered was simple and consistent: the beginning of wisdom is to know thyself, and the temperate life was the ideal. For the Greeks the person of wisdom is the one who devotes all of one's energies in inquiring about the self. This self-knowledge was matured by the virtue of temperance which allowed one to know the limits of the self and not seek to transgress what Fate or the gods has pre-established. Prometheus stood as a reminder for those who wanted to be like the gods and play with fire. Self-knowledge was not the radical individualism or "me-ness" that we experience today. Plato and Aristotle reminded the citizenry that self-knowledge and development were to take place in the city (polis) with one's fellows. To be human is to be social.

The Hebrew tradition concerning wisdom is expressed in the writings of the wiseman Ben-Sirach. Wisdom for the Hebrew comes through fear of the Lord. The fear of which the Bible speaks is akin to awe or reverence when one encounters Yahweh as the Wholly Other and essence of Holiness. Wisdom brings happiness (blessedness) and inner harmony. Wisdom is not easily acquired but requires discipline, sacrifice, and obedience. Wisdom is not a possession, but a process that strips away the illusions that cover the self's fundamental covenant relationship with Yahweh. The Hebrew notion of wisdom makes room for the Laws and the witness of creation. The Law reveals the wise will of Yahweh and what he expects for his people. Creation is the work of Yahweh's hands and serves as a living testimony to the power and love of God. Above all, the Hebrew experience of wisdom is one of mystery which man must encounter through silence and in wonder.

The God for Every Day

The Greek and Hebrew traditions of wisdom converge at this crucial point: wisdom is essential to virtue and virtue enriches wisdom. Wisdom is related to man's quest for self-understanding, growth as a human being, and the possibility of living harmoniously within the state or with Someone—Yahweh. Greek and Hebrew wisdom require the discipline of self-examination, questioning, and openness to the word of others and the word of the Lord. Today humankind has forgotten that wisdom is related to virtue and authentic knowledge is subjective, that is, related to the self. Today wisdom has become knowledge centered on facts in an abstract way and unrelated to the developing self. In effect, wisdom is stripped of virtue and we are left with knowledge as *power*. Knowledge has lost its ethical base and has forgotten its twin subjects: God and the self. Such a loss of memory disrupts the social bond of justice and love between individuals and communities. The quest for knowledge as power eliminates the ethical and transcendental dimensions, and hands knowledge over to technological imperatives guided by the individualized ego. The "will to power," to dominate, and control is all too present in our own epoch. On a large scale such power is given expression in the nationalistic, militaristic, and imperialistic imperatives of modern nation-states. The sphere of interpersonal relationships seems to be no better. In the modern industrial state my fellow man is not my neighbor to whom I owe the debt of love, but rather he is my competitor, adversary, and in the end, becomes my enemy who is trying to grasp the bread from my table. Man's relationship with the self has been distorted as well. We are a generation of the "Lonely Crowd" and the radically individualized "Me-Generation". Man no longer views the self related to the community in cooperation, and we often fail to experience community in our daily living. We have sown the winds of privacy and individual rights. We must now reap the whirlwind of loneliness and alienation.

In recent times our consciousness has been raised concerning our violent and irreverent relationship with nature. Creation and nature have lost their sacramental power in the modern period. Creation is no longer a portal to God, but is viewed simply as a *means* to some technological end. Creation has become demythified and with that loss of mystery and sacredness, man's world has become poorer; and man as well. Creation is no longer the story of God's power and love, but is the passive stuff on which man works his technological will. It is beginning to dawn on us that the reality of a cold ecological nightmare can be just as real and frightening as a nuclear holocaust. Nature is not

passive or indifferent to our willfulness and ir-
reverence. Arrogance and pride exact their
price. Smog and pollution of the air are only the
initial downpayments.

Does all of this mean that despair is our
response to the whole mess? If one claims to be a
Christian the answer must be a resounding *NO!*
The response of the Christian is always one of
hope. Hope is not optimism which often demands
immediate results in order to be sustained. Optimism often turns to despair because it is not
demanding and tough enough to endure. Hope,
on the other hand, is faith thrust to the future.
Hope does not demand instant results. Hope is
sustained by the power of the future who is God.
Hope is above all the active work of the Holy
Spirit within us and the world. Man's hope for
much needed wisdom is found in the Spirit working through memory and creative imagination.
The Spirit or Paraclete works through memory
helping us to recollect and recover the past.
Memory is not a reactionary faculty that freezes
life. Quite the contrary. Memory is our link with
all those who have gone before and struggled to
make our lot more human. Memory is essential
to identity and sanity. Memory is the storehouse
of experience which helps us to navigate in the
present and project a future. The Spirit helps us
to recall the essentials of life, that is, what God
has done for us; what God expects of us; and

above all what God hopes for us. The Paraclete works through our creative imagination and helps us to envision that which could be. The Paraclete liberates our intellect to transcend the present and peer, however imperfectly, into the future; and always with hope. The Spirit is the wisdom of Jesus at work within us and our world. The Paraclete is the reminder that all that we have and are results from the love of God. The Paraclete reminds us that we are meant to live in community with love for our neighbor. The Paraclete keeps us in the truth about our stewardship concerning nature. Man is called to be a co-creator, but never to become so proud that man's creatureliness is forgotten. The Paraclete is the inner light and wisdom of God present within to guide and gladden us. The Paraclete as the Power of Hope shines in the darkness of our present hour. We must hope this and believe this. We do. Lord help our unbelief.

Up to this point in our discussion we have spoken about God in the context of everyday life. We have attempted to apply the experience and testimony of the early Church that God is Father (with us), Son (for us), and Spirit (within us) to the demands of our existence and the contemporary situation. We have done this on the conviction that God is all in all, and we can only live authentically to the degree that we are open to him and his presence in our life. As we approach the final section of our inquiry we want to extend this experience of God to some of the more enduring themes in Christian life. Namely, we want to reflect on the world, community, prayer, faith, and the style in which the Christian is called to make his or her presence felt in the everyday world. We will examine each of these concerns in light of our everyday God and his love for us. In the words of the beloved New Orleans poet Jim Metcalf, "please to begin."

PART IV
Everyday Concerns

The World

RELATIONSHIP and language are two great essentials of human living. To be human is to be in relationship and to speak a language. The first three sections of our inquiry have been an attempt to speak to God in the language of our everyday concerns. The God who revealed himself and emptied himself in Jesus is the God who is made present to us in the words of ordinary and routine existence. It is crucial that we speak about God in such ordinary and familiar terms. God is the Ground, Redeemer, and Omega of our most public and private moments. God cannot be banished to specific places or times such as a church building for fifty-minutes on a Sunday. The revelation of God who is the Lord of History breaks the chains of cultural and personal custom and reasserts that he is the Lord of the Everyday as well. God will not be bought off by our liturgical sacrifices or pious lip service. The God for Everyday is much more demanding than that. What does God want of us? "This is what God asks of you, only this: to act justly, to love tenderly, and to walk humbly with your God" (Micah 6:8). The God who has spoken and revealed himself in word, deed, and flesh con-

tinues to lure his creation to its fulfillment through the daily existence of the Christian in the marketplace. The world is not the product of the blind forces of nature, but creation is the work of God's hands and he proclaims it to be good. The world cannot run on a logic of its own independent of the One who creates, redeems, and sustains. The creation is God's creation and the Christian is called to be actively present in its transformation so that God is all in all. Jesus tells his disciples they will not be removed from the world; quite the opposite, they must remain in the world so that proper glory can be given to the Father. The disciples of Jesus, in all places and for all times, are living symbols of what God has done in Jesus and continues to do until his fullness extends to the whole of creation. The Christian does not seek to flee from the world. The Christian realizes that he or she is in the world and called to transform it.

The critical reader will no doubt object at this point and say that the world is part of the demonic forces which wage war against God's kingdom. The world is part of that Unholy Alliance, along with the flesh and the devil, which condemned Jesus to death and frustrates God's will. To a great extent this is true. Scripture does speak about the world in rather disparaging terms. The world in Scripture is understood in two ways: metaphysically and sacramentally.

The world does have a sinister side and is understood as the forces of evil, held under the sway of Satan, which seek to obstruct the Divine Will. This metaphysical understanding of the world, as the power of darkness, is all too real and cannot be trivialized or demythologized away. The world hates Jesus and those who come in his name (Jn. 15:18). However, this is only part of Scripture's understanding of the world. The world as creation is the work of God's hands and is declared to be good. The world comes into being through the creative love of the Word. The world is in effect a sacrament, that is, a window and revelation of God's Beauty, Goodness, and Truth. The world speaks to humankind of the God who so loved the world that he sent his only Son to be its redeemer and hope (Jn. 3:16). The Christian shares that vocation of love toward the world and, at the same time, knows well that part of the world which obscures God's loving presence. The Christian disciple is challenged to make God's work his or her own, that is, speak the Word of Life to the world and work to make it more just and sensitive to its true identity as God's work of creative love. We cannot opt for God *and* the world. No doubt the relationship we have with the world causes tension. We feel the need to embrace the world and see it as God's cosmic gift to us. The world also is experienced as that which so often hides God and his will.

The evil, banality, and senseless waste and in-humanity have caused many to cry, "God is Dead!" We feel the temptation to repudiate the world and all its ugliness. We want to say "God only" and yet this cannot be done. Creation also mourns for the lost Good and eagerly anticipates the second coming of the Risen One. In other words, humankind and the world are in need of redemption and healing. The destiny of man and the world converge in the shadow of the Cross and the hope of an empty tomb.

If the individual Christian or the community of Christians we call the Church, rejects the world then in a real sense the Divine Commission of Jesus is likewise rejected. The individual Chris-tian and the churches have a mission to the world given by the Risen and Ascended Lord himself: "You will be my witnesses not only in Jerusalem but throughout Judea and Samaria, and indeed to the ends of the earth" (Acts 1:8). The disciples in Acts and each new generation of Christians, are called to venture forth into the world and proclaim what God has done, is now doing, and what God will do in the future. We cannot escape such a mission and commission and be true to our Christian identity. The more telling criticisms leveled against religion and the Churches are brought to bear by those who ac-cuse religion of becoming an ideology or opium. Religion and the churches falsify consciousness and legitimate unjust structures and political elites when they become too closely identified with a particular historical power arrangement. Religion and the churches become instruments of oppression and tools in the hands of those whose only interest is the entrenchment of their own power. This ideological wedding of church and state is not just a fact of the medieval world, but was present in Nazi Germany and is present today when churches and Christians fail to speak and act on behalf of those who are powerless and without anyone to plead their cause. It should not be silent. God speaks for the alien, orphan, unborn, powerless, and the elderly.

The churches and religion can also escape responsibility by fostering a spirituality which encourages one to flee from the world and think only of "pie in the sky when you die." Both the oppressed and oppressor are excused from the demands of justice. The oppressed are given good marks if they silently endure sinful social structures. The oppressor is never called to conversion and a change of heart. The *status quo* is blessed and everyone is cursed. The spirituality which encourages such a radical other-worldly orientation often leads to that which most severely limits the effectiveness of Christian witness: the privatization of the gospel. The churches speak a ghetto language and operate in the subjective sandbox of the individual's beach or particular church. Often the call to conversion never extends beyond the church doors or one's private room. In Part One (God with Us) we spoke of sin and asked if one could sin any more. We need to further and extend our reflections by saying, yes one can sin, and sin is not only a personal or private affair. Sin is social and has community consequences. Sin is not only my personal and knowing free-will violations of relationship with God and neighbor, but sin is also those alienating and oppressive structures which rob people of the essentials of well being. These alienating and oppressive structures foster a deceptive consciousness in which one is blind to injustice and brutality. It is not that the rich man in the parable of Jesus actively hurt the beggar at his gate, but the rich man was blind and insensitive to his needs. The cry of the poor and the evidence of need could not find their way into the heart of the one who lived and feasted splendidly each day. The privatization of the gospel does just that, namely, blinds us and makes us insensitive to the needs of those around us. The gospel becomes an ideology and Jesus is used as an instrument for legitimating the powers that be.

In order to overcome the temptation to turn the gospel into an ideology and a private affair we must remember that conversion is social as well as private. Jesus enters Galilee and proclaims the need for repentance because the kingdom of God is at hand. God's kingdom is one of justice, mercy, and peace. The gospel conversion that Jesus proclaims calls for a critical examination of the various institutions that comprise our social world. God creates, lives, and redeems the world. The kingdom of God stands as the ultimate critique of the various social arrangements in which we live. The need to recognize that the gospel can be misused and turned into an ideology or become privatized is not advanced only by those who oppose religion. This recognition of gospel misuse is also being voiced by the so-called liberation and black theologians. These men and women are articulating the cries of the oppressed and marginals in our world. They are reminding us that to be a Christian is to be a witness to the Lord of History and the God for Everyday in transforming the world. Their words can be uncomfortable and disturbing, especially when they remind us that the churches are in need of conversion as well.

Prophetic words are never easy, but that makes them all the more necessary. This is not to say that everyone who wraps himself or herself in the garment of liberation has a privileged input to God and absolute truth. We know all too well how liberation has a way of becoming a new and often worse form of enslavement. The gospel criteria for all who claim to work in God's name is the fruit that is produced. True gospel liberation has as its goal the ultimate reconciliation of the various elements in society so that peace and justice can be more meaningfully experienced. No social structure, however enlightened or well intended, will be perfect. That will only come with the final, definitive rule of God. Until that time beyond time we are called to work, struggle, and hope; above all, we work in hope. The churches do not have all the answers, and they need to listen and learn from those who possess the necessary technical and professional skills in the areas of politics, economics, education and the like. What the churches do bring is the critical and prophetic voice of the gospel which reminds all, that apart from God and his will there is no scheduled part of life. Economics and politics have moral implications and these implications come under the discernment of the gospel.

It is sometimes said that religion and politics don't mix; church and state are to be forever separate. Such a view only further privatizes the gospel and renders the mission of the church to the world "a noisy gong or a clashing cymbal." As we move through a new decade and beyond, high on the church's agenda will be the need to speak about God in an authentic and meaningful way. Our God-talk must pay more than lip-service to the vocal cries of desperate lives both within and outside the churches. The church has already made evangelization a weighty issue. Evangelism is the recognition that the church and each Christian have a fundamental relationship with the world. Evangelization is the call from the church for the church to be the church, that is, the redeeming, transforming presence of God in his world. If evangelization is to be more than a fad or "the noise of solemn assemblies" we must reaffirm our mission to the world and work to liberate all peoples from those structures which render life short, brutish, and cruel. We must once again dedicate ourselves to building a world after the heart of Yahweh:

> Hate evil and love good,
> and let justice prevail at the
> gate; . . . if you would offer
> me holocausts, then let justice
> surge like water, and goodness
> like an unfailing stream.
> (Am. 5:15; 24)

Coercion or Persuasion?

IN the previous chapter we indicated that the Christian cannot choose God or the world, rather, the Christian is related to God *and* the world. The Christian is called to share in God's work of transforming the world into a more just and God-present entity. It must also be said that one cannot be either a Christian or a member of a given society. The Christian is located in a world, a social context, and this world or context influences the shape of Christianity. Likewise, Christianity helps to shape the given society. We are Christians and Americans, and each influences the other. There is a definite "American Christianity" and it is important to be sensitive to the extent to which culture influences religion and *vice versa*. We Americans are an active lot. We must be up and doing. This action orientation towards life has its roots in the very foundation of the Republic. When our ancestors first arrived on these shores what was needed were men and women of action and practical skills. The forest had to be cleared, food gathered, crops planted, houses built, and defenses against hostile forces and people erected. In such a world theory enjoys little cash value.

What come to be valued are pragmatic skills and ideas which have effective consequences in the real world. The original contribution of the American intellectual community to philosophy is *pragmatism*. This system of philosophy was developed by Charles Sanders Peirce, who held that the worth of a belief was determined by its consequences or results. If the desired results were achieved the belief worked; if not, the belief should be discarded. To many intellectual purists such a philosophical stance was barbaric; however, pragmatism fit beautifully with the American experience. The Christian is part of this active and pragmatic orientation to life. We cannot shed our cultural skins as easily as the snake sheds its skin. Culture is a type of second nature to us and it derives its power by working on us in often unconscious or pre-reflective ways. We take for granted as part of everyday reality the values, hopes, and judgments of the society in which we live. These taken for granted elements cannot be limited to so-called secular concerns only, as they also influence and shape the style of religious value and expression. It is necessary to mention the influence of culture on religion since in our last chapter we expressed the belief that the Christian is called to be active and work for the transformation of the world. In many ways our previous reflections could be interpreted to be very American. After all, Americans have always liked action and the challenge of transforming the world. The call to transform the world can be seen as the clarion call to get the job done with typical American compulsion and know-how. However, this is not quite what is meant. The call to transform the world for justice does not flow from a manifest destiny of a political sort, but flows from two inter-related sources: the nature of God and his style of relating to the world, and secondly, from the structure of Christian existence, that is, *being* Christian in the world.

Classical theology often speaks about God's *agency* in the world. Agency is used to express the way(s) in which God works, relates, and generally makes his presence felt and his will known to the world. There are two general ways in which God has been experienced as acting in the world: coercion and persuasion. Many of the early religions of humankind understood God to be a coercive being. Such a god demanded sacrifice (often of the human variety) and worship, or dire consequences would follow. For instance, the Nile would flood and the crops be destroyed if proper reverence was not paid the gods. Sacrifice and worship were used to buy-off the gods and keep their sensitive egos from being bruised. The coercive god was also an unpredictable sort and, therefore, daily existence was filled with tension. One never knew what to expect next, or what was expected of one.

However, the Israelites experienced Yahweh in a different way. Yahweh could get angry, jealous, and cause havoc (the Flood, Sodom and Gomorrah, Lot's wife were not to be taken lightly), but on the whole, Yahweh was a God of love, compassion, and justice. Yahweh was holy and demanded that his people be holy. Yahweh could not be bribed with sacrifices and cult offerings. Only a pure heart and a people dedicated to justice could enjoy a covenant relationship with Yahweh. The writers of the Old Testament experienced Yahweh in a rather ambivalent way, but overall they knew that Yahweh was concerned about them and was concerned about the ways in which they related to each other. Yahweh sent the prophets to remind, exhort, and call the people back to him and the covenant. Only as a last resort did Yahweh's anger blaze and destruction (the Babylonian Exile for example) befall the People. Even then, however, Yahweh refused to abandon the Vine he took out of Egypt and planted in a land of milk and honey (Ps. 80). Yahweh always offers life and hope to those who repent. In other words, Yahweh only uses coercion when all else fails, and even then, he still offers the opportunity to re-enter the covenant relationship. Yahweh is not experienced as a God of coercion, but as a God who passionately cares for his people.

So much does Yahweh care for his world that "in the fullness of time" he speaks his ultimate Word who dwells among us and we behold the very nature and agency of God. In Jesus we experience the definitive revelation of *who* God is and *what* God is about. In Jesus we come to experience God as our Father whose very nature is suffering, enduring love; "grace following upon grace." In Jesus we come to experience how God is really at work in the world, namely, as Divine Persuasion. Jesus reveals to us that the Really Real is a Tender Poet who calls all of creation to life in abundance. In the words of A. N. Whitehead, Jesus reveals to us that God is our "fellow sufferer and companion; the one who understands." Recent trends in theology and science have indicated how important models are for articulating the essentials of each discipline. Science makes fruitful use of what are called picture or theoretical models. Such models are mental constructions which provide one with an intellectual picture of the basic elements of the physical world. Examples of such intellectual picture models would be the atom, an electron, or even black holes in space. Theologian David Tracy indicates that theology makes use of a different sort of model, namely, disclosure models.

Disclosure models are not exact, clear and distinct pictures of reality, but they help us to understand fundamental aspects of human behavior. Disclosure models highlight and bring to illumination key aspects of our being-in-the-world. One example of a disclosure model would be original sin which helps to explain, however imperfectly, the finitude and limitations of existence. Disclosure models need not be limited only to mythic symbols, but certain persons can serve as a disclosure model to help us understand fundamental elements of reality and human existence. Jesus is the disclosure model who reveals the very nature of God as love and proclaims that God wants to draw and lure all of creation into the Divine Nature. In Jesus we see that God accomplishes this luring task by the persuasive power of love; even if that demands the ultimate sacrifice.

In the life of Jesus we experience all the tender elements of the world and the willingness of God to suffer with and for his creation. The disclosure of God as Divine Persuasion and the Tender Poet who lures the world toward its full realization, is expressed with beauty and power in the Parable of the Prodigal Son (Forgiving Father) and ultimately by Jesus on the Cross. It is to St. Luke that we owe a debt of gratitude for preserving the parable of the Prodigal Son (Lk. 15:11-32). The so-called prodigal or lost son feels the need to do his own thing and travel to a distant land. This desire indicates that the son is in the grip of sin because he wants to break relationship. The father does not protest or threaten, but he allows his son to make this necessary journey of self-discovery. After experiencing a reversal of fortune the son comes to his senses (the power of grace) and decides to return home. This takes great courage on the part of the son and is a magnificent testimony to how strong he believes his father to be. In effect, the son believes that his father is strong enough to be tender and forgiving. When the father sees the son he rejoices and welcomes him home. Persuasion and grace have won out over coercion and law. The second son, who is really the prodigal or lost son, cannot accept what has happened and refuses to enter and celebrate. The second son has served, or better, slaved for his father out of a distorted, stale sense of duty. However, the second son has never loved his father, brother, or ultimately himself. The second son operates by coercion and a legalism which kills the Spirit. We are left to wonder if the second son was ever able to go in and rejoice. Jesus tells parables to surprise and shock his audience out of their taken-for-granted and all too smug world. One would expect the Father to command his son to stay home, or if he does leave he is never to return. The attitude of the second son is what the audience expected. However, Jesus subverts the obvious and invites the audience to be surprised by the ways of God. This parable indicates that God's ways cannot be programmed or limited by human expectations, and in the final analysis it is persuasion that returns the lost to their home and brings the dead back to life.

It is ultimately in the Cross and the "Man of Sorrows" that the definitive revelation of God's nature and agency is made visible for all to see with the eye of faith. The Cross is the crucified God's throne. His crown is thorns and he rules with a power that transcends Rome and the kingdom of Caesar. From the Cross, God in Jesus draws all things to himself by the power of suffering, enduring love. To be sure not everyone recognized the Lordship of Jesus. As his life ebbed away the taunts and skepticism of the crowd persisted. Certainly in our own day the Cross continues to be foolishness and a stumbling block. But to each generation who walk by faith the Cross is the power and wisdom of God. In Jesus and the drama of the cross we experience each man's struggle with the ultimate question of existence. In Jesus, suspended between heaven and earth, we witness the one who continues to hope and forgive even as the forces of death and darkness gather all around. In Jesus we witness a life that was lived in total openness to God as Father, and on the cross that life is consummated by a surrender of ultimate hope and trust. The Cross speaks to every person about the real possibility for authentic existence, that is, an existence that is expressed in openness and surrender to the unconditional mystery we call God. The Cross is God's word that he stands with man in all of his tragedy and fallenness and still calls forth the hope of new life. In the midst of suffering, banality, indifference, hatred, and the forces of evil so powerful that the sun must shut its eyes and the earth spew forth the dead, God is most especially there doing the work of redemption. God is there not in majesty and pomp; not protesting and pleading; but God is there in a man who prays for forgiveness for those who know not what they do. God is present as the one who promises to those who ask that they too will share in paradise. God is present as the one who thirsts, and will continue to thirst, until all of creation accomplishes what is most difficult and most necessary: surrender into the unbounded love of God. In the drama of the Cross and the obscured victory of the tomb, God answers for all time what is the Really Real, namely, that the nature of God is love and the God who is love makes his presence felt through the Divine Persuasion of Love.

What does the experience of God as Divine

Persuasion, who is and acts through love, have to say to the one who claims to *be* Christian? In other words, what is disclosed about the very structure of Christian existence through God's presence in Jesus? The presence of God in Jesus tells us that Christian existence is grounded in the power of persuasion over coercion and enduring love over raw force. Before the Christian acts in the world he or she must experience what it means *to be*. Christian action flows from the structure of Christian existence or being. This revelation of persuasion over coercion by Jesus is crucial for the mission of the community we call church and the everyday life of the Christian in the world.

The Cross serves as the ultimate reminder to the Christian community that its power is derived from love and the ability to persuade and suffer with others. The more tragic chapters of Christian history were written by those who sought to use force in seeking to bring about the Kingdom of God. The Crusades, the Inquisition, religious wars, and missionary imperialism all attest to the limitations and futility of force as the ultimate answer to the world's problems. By contrast, the Christian community has been most Christ-like when it has spoken and acted with love and humility. The Christian community has been and will be most itself as the abiding presence of God in the world, to the extent that it seeks to lure the world by the persuasive power of love. This is not easy. It calls for the churches to be willing to suffer with their own limitations, immaturity, and sinfulness as well as that of the whole world. But this is precisely the scandal of the Cross: love does not mean you never say you're sorry, rather, love is the willingness to suffer with and for the other, all the while hoping for victory. Persuasion demands that the churches be strong enough to be tender and, above all, patient. This is especially challenging to those whose ministry touches the least of our brothers and sisters in poor and Third World countries. Powerful forces are at work which proclaim the sword and the need to send fire upon the earth. Are there times when coercion and violence must be used? Coercion is the last resort in a fallen world with a tragic history. Those who must resort to coercion should always do so with a sense of deep contrition and a recognition of failure. For every display of coercion is not a show of power but of weakness. Love and reason have failed and the power of darkness has once again had its hour. But even in the midst of violence and coercion God is there, too, working to salvage what is noble and heal what is broken. The power of God is his ability to transform the darkness into a light that will not be overcome.

The structure of individual Christian existence or being is based on the same principle of Divine Persuasion and love disclosed by Jesus and expressed in the Parable of the Prodigal Son. In the landscape of our interpersonal lives there is much tragedy and human wreckage. The fatalities and waste are often the result of our desire to show the other who is boss or who has more ego-strength. In other words, the defeats and pain of our interpersonal lives often result because we have opted for coercion over persuasion. And why not, one can legitimately ask? After all, no one wants to get stepped on or be labeled as a push-over. We must assert our rights, stand our ground, and defend our turf at all cost. And yet in our more sober moments we see, however much through a glass only dimly, the pain and waste that has resulted from a macho or coercive approach to others. Often coercion and loud talk serve as masks for fear which keeps persuasion and love in check. The forgiving father in our parable refuses to play the "hard-to-get" game.

The father was overjoyed that the lost son had been found; the dead restored to life. He couldn't be restrained by the conventional wisdom which demands an apology, calls for the other to crawl back, or ultimately refuses to ever enter into relationship again. In our own society we witness the pain and destruction caused in families where coercion and not per-

suasion is the guiding principle of relationships.
Each year all too many children run away from
home and travel to a distant land. The divorce
rate in American society has approached fifty
percent. There has been an alarming rise in the
number of teenage alcoholics, teenage preg-
nancies, not to mention the persistence of a
drug culture that will not go away. One can only
wonder how often a significant cause for each
of these is a failure for those involved to relate
to each other from a stance of persuasion and
enduring love. Such a persuasive love demands
that one set aside the prerogative of status and
age and listen to the other in spirit and truth.
However, the forces of coercion are strong and
numerous reasons can be advanced which will
make the persuasive love of Christian existence
seem foolish or idealistic. The attempt to under-
mine persuasion did not surprise Jesus for he
knew what was in man's heart and how the majority love darkness rather than light. However,
there are enough moments in our personal and
collective history when the light shines in the
darkness of fear and coercion. There are enough
moments when the weapons of interpersonal
combat are disarmed and we stand vulnerable
before the other. This takes great courage and
the strength to hope. It is not a courage and hope
we produce on our own. Ultimately it is God's
grace at work in the "Man of Sorrows" and in

the lives of those who are born in the shadow of the Cross and exist daily in the hope of Easter.

The foundation of Christian existence as persuasion has a strange ring to the ears of those whose marketplace is America. The crucial lessons of Vietnam are painful for Americans to learn, namely, that power and coercion have their limits. This is especially true of military and economic power. We cannot bomb people into democracy and we cannot buy friends who will be loyal and noble. The contemporary world has rejected all policemen. However, the big-stick approach to international relations is tempting, especially in this post-Vietnam era. Many want to forget what happened in Vietnam; never mind that the suppression of such events often invites them to recur with greater tragedy. The individual Christian and the churches are called to work for peace and justice. We can make a significant contribution to the American experience by living and proclaiming the need for a human world order that rests on persuasive love. Such efforts will no doubt be misunderstood and at times met with opposition. However, we should not be deterred, but continue to work, believe, and hope that God's work has become our own.

Community:
But Can I Still Be Me?

IN our first two sections we advanced the position that the Christian is in the world and called to transform the world for justice and peace. The Christian is challenged to work for world transformation through the power of persuasion, enduring love and not through coercion and violence. In effect, our reflections have been leading to the position that the Christian is called to build communities of care and respect for the dignity and sacredness of each person. It is to this understanding and experience of Christian community that we now turn our attention.

If there is one feature of contemporary life that is a heavy yoke and makes itself felt, it is that of the *bigness* of life. Our everyday world is surrounded by institutions which structure our world and too often seem to be on the verge of swallowing us up. There is big government, business, unions, and even churches—yes, big churches in which we can feel the cold isolation and anonymity as much as factory workers in a General Motors plant. There are few issues which can claim consensus in our pluralistic and special issue oriented society. However, one issue does so—namely that modern life is too cold and remote from the everyday needs and concerns of the proverbial man (and of course, woman!) in the street. It is hard not to feel that *The Lonely Crowd* is our biography and we are the organizational people of the grey flannel suit brigade. Urban crime runs rampant in the steel canyons of our cities because no one wants to get involved. The cities of America are the graduate schools of crime and violence in which the criminal can roam free knowing that the chance that he will be called to the bar of justice is remote. The young reject the traditional institutional forms of religion as hypocritical and insensitive to their concerns. The young flock in large numbers to join various religious cults which demand discipline and sacrifice, all the while offering what young people are most hungry for: a fundamental meaning for everyday existence and a sense of belonging to something bigger than the imperial self, that is, one can *belong* to a community. It is easier, and a lot less troubling, to denounce the young as immature, idealistic, or even godless, and the leaders of the various cults as manipulators, rather than face the hard reality that these cults are in fact articulating and responding to genuine human needs. These religious cults have taken seriously the wisdom of Aristotle and the instruction of the Scriptures, that is, to be human is to be a social being who needs the company of his fellows.

The need for community and to experience caring relationships is not the unique need of the young, but extends throughout our society and certainly speaks to the everyday concerns of the elderly. It is not easy to be old in a society that worships the young and honors the Pepsi Generation as the ideal. Psychiatrist Erik Erikson speaks about old age as the stage of integrity in which one can sum up and reflect back upon one's existence and pronounce one's life as good. However, this is increasingly difficult in a society which measures worth in terms of the power to consume, spend, and produce. The elderly are often on fixed incomes which limit their economic clout. In addition, the elderly are more prone to sickness and injury which limit their capacity to produce. American society encourages children to "fly from the nest" as a sign of maturity and make a life of their own. The long distance phone call is not the next best thing to being there, it is often the only way for the elderly to be with their children or relatives. Fear of violence often makes the elderly prisoners in their own homes. The elderly experience, with each passing day, the cold grip of loneliness and neglect. In highlighting the young and the elderly we cannot overlook those in the middle course of life who feel that opportunity and fulfillment have passed them by and so they must turn to desperate sexual adventures to bolster a sagging ego. If sex is not the answer there is often alcohol and drugs to numb the pain. All in all, it is hard to deny that the need for community and a sense of belonging is crucial for an everyday existence which transcends the sociological factors of status, class, race, and religion.

Since so many are in agreement concerning the need for community and belonging, why have effective caring communities been so difficult to form? No doubt urbanization and industrialization have done much to splinter families and isolate large segments of the population. The invention of the automobile and its essential place in our everyday routine, has made us a society on wheels that offers us almost unlimited freedom. However, the automobile has also exaggerated loneliness and the rootlessness of our mobile society. In the words of Vance Packard, we are a "nation of strangers." There are deeper causes at work which make the building of community so hard to come by. There are elements in the American experience and psyche which make Americans ambivalent, if not downright hostile. We Americans first and foremost value our *freedom*. Community has a way of limiting our liberty and the achievement of our individual goals. Others have a way of narrowing our future options and placing obstacles in the path of our mobility.

In the American mind freedom is related to the experience of *space*. We are used to vast, unlimited space which has become idealized in the myth of the frontier. Vast space speaks to us of unlimited opportunity and more importantly, of our ability to escape the restraints of civilization and our own past sins or failures. We can always move on and start anew in the vast land of opportunity. Americans view space not merely in geographical terms as the distance between points on a map, but as a psychological and moral quality. Space is not only the distance between towns, it is the distance between individuals which highlights loneliness.

This brings us to the third element which makes community building difficult, namely, this need to be unattached and mobile through vast spaces gives rise to the American hero as a loner. The American hero is a-historical and unattached. He has no past: he simply is and comes upon the scene to right a wrong and always he must move on. The American hero cannot be encumbered by interpersonal relationships and the bonds of community. The American hero is a wanderer on the face of the earth. Rarely is he on the side of law and convention, rather, he is the one who challenges and strikes out at the injustices that press in on others. Even when he is cloaked with the symbols of civilization he acts in a most unconventional way. The American hero seeks to escape his past sins by moving on to the next challenge.

The archetype of the American hero is *Shane* who comes out of nowhere, fights the forces of evil, and has to move on: for the settled life is not in the cards. The cries of "come back Shane, come back" do not touch the heart of the American Adam. The media heroes who flood the television scene are almost always men who are self-reliant, single or alone, strong, and without a past (Jack Lord of Hawaii Five-O on television and the movie characters played by Clint Eastwood serve as excellent examples of the American hero). In varying degrees the American hero lives within each of us.

The Judeo-Christian symbol system has much to offer in healing the pain of loneliness and the building of caring communities. The Judeo-Christian tradition has always asserted that God called *a people* and not just individuals, to be his own. The Israelites in the Old Testament were chosen to be the People of the Covenant through whom every nation would receive a blessing (Gen. 12:2-3). In the New Testament Jesus calls the Twelve, a community of friends, who are to live and love as Jesus loved them. The community, gathering, or church is born from the Cross with the handing over of the Spirit. Fear and disillusionment give way to the bold proclamation of what God has done in Jesus. The church, the gathering together of a people, comes into existence as a community that is united in its experience and profession of Jesus as Lord. In the Crucified and Risen One, the community comes to experience the answer to the fundamental questions of human existence. To believe in Jesus is to be part of a people who live, move, and have their being through a common relationship in the Lord. It is a community existence that does not seek to destroy individuality and creativity, but strives to promote what is best in each person. Freedom, individuality, and talents are always developed in a social context or community. The community is necessary for social involvement in the issues of peace and justice. A community response is necessary if social injustice and sin structure are to be reformed. Nazism, for example, could not have been counteracted by individual action alone. What was needed was action by the world community and the community witness of various churches. The community of solidarity in the Lord stands as a challenge to the rugged individualism and egoism that is so destructive to human growth. In addition, the community serves as a reality principle which challenges any one member from claiming a special corner on the truth.

Truth is social and part of a tradition and not a private affair in the doing of one's own thing. All that we have said so far about community is not to suggest that "the little flock" called by the Good Shepherd is perfect and in possession of absolute truth. The triumphal church should be allowed to rest in peace. The community which gathers to remember the Lord in the breaking of bread and the hearing of the Word is itself in need of conversion and healing. The Christian community is never above its own proclamation, but is a good teacher to the extent that it also listens and learns. If we are not advocating the triumphal church neither must we give in to the "doom-boom" despair and hopelessness about the real, here and now church. We are called to love, hope, and struggle within the one and only community we have. To that sinful, limited, imperfect, and wart-covered bride we are wedded in hope. Not a hope of our own doing or achievements, but the hope that is found in the One who died and now lives.

The Christian understanding of community speaks with power and meaning to two of the more important concerns of the American experience: pluralism and a suspicious relationship toward authority.

1. *Pluralism.* One of the most unique features of the American landscape is the tremendous diversity which characterizes so much of our everyday—race, religion, ethnic origins, and political performances. This diversity or pluralism has strong ties to the beginning of the Republic when our Founding Fathers sought to ensure that no one religious group would gain

control of the helm of the ship. But more importantly, pluralism is considered the great and crowning achievement of the American experiment in freedom. In America one can be a nonconformist and still make it big. In fact, we honor and revere those who are unconventional. We respect and reward those who "march to a different drummer" and follow the music they hear, however much it diverges from the well worn path. Pluralism is viewed as the essential ingredient and sign that the American experience is successful. Pluralism tells the world that there is room for all people and in *this* land even the downtrodden, the poor, and the rejected of the world can be transformed and made anew. We take pride not so much in royalty and the achievements of birth as in the ability of the individual to work and contribute to the common good that is the American way of life. Pluralism is the essential of freedom, mobility, and what it means to live in America. Community is often viewed with reservation since individual initiative and drive must be subordinated at times to the good of others. We often view community as the enemy and stumbling block to authentic personal growth. It is at this point the Christian would like to offer a word about the relationship between the individual and the community.

The Christian understanding of community

does not negate the efforts, talents, skills, and authentic existence of the individual—just the opposite. Community is essential if one is to achieve one's potential and others are necessary if one is to even come to a recognition of the gifts one does possess. The Apostle Paul, in his first letter to the Corinthians (Chapter 12). offers us an insightful model for protecting the value of the individual while working for the common good or community goals. This model is that of the human body. The Corinthians were very much like we Americans—talented, resourceful, diverse, intelligently creative, and possessing a great love for debating the latest political and religious issues. However, this creativity and diversity had its dark side, namely, it was undermining their essential unity with one another in the Lord. The destructive forces of factionalism, rivalry, jealousy, and insensitivity were characterizing their social gatherings; most especially their Eucharistic celebrations. Paul, showing deep pastoral concern, wants to make sure that their diversity and giftedness does not become the very source of their destruction.

Paul reminds them that all their gifts and talents (wisdom, knowledge, faith, healing, prophecy, discernment of spirits, speaking in tongues, and the interpretation of tongues) come from the Spirit and are given for the common good. If disunity and brokenness are to be kept to a minimum they must remember that each gift is not a possession for personal glory but is to be used as a blessing for all. The human body is one though it has many parts. Each part is necessary for health and life. No one part can be excluded if the body is to mature. Each part contributes in accordance to its nature or function. The body is weakened to the extent that any of its members is ill or not properly functioning as a part of the whole. The body image illustrates the need for unity *and* diversity—the need for each member to contribute and be a part of the whole.

The community is the body writ large. Just like the body, if a community is to grow it must creatively use the gifts and talents of *all* its people for the common good. The caring community is the one which allows all of its members to freely experience their creative gifts for the good of the whole. In that way individuality is protected while at the same time the social aspects of life are enriched. However, the caring community is more than a sociological entity or a gathering of individuals in pursuit of a common goal or interest. The caring community is a *moral* entity which seeks to creatively invite and make sure that the dignity and sacredness of the individual is safeguarded. In the moral, caring community the individual is never a *means* only to some end, but is always an *end*. The caring community operates by the principle of *inclusion* which reaches out to all and yet always respects the freedom of the one to say his or her No.

Membership in the community of care is not dependent upon social utility or the power to consume or produce. The moral thrust of the caring community is exhibited by actively seeking out the marginals and powerless and baptizing them with the waters of new life, anointing them with the oil of gladness, and extending the kiss of peace. Such a community takes on itself a special responsibility of gathering into its fold those who feel most out of it. The brokenness of the sick, the poverty of the poor, and the despair of the marginals are made the concern of the community. Likewise, the resources of the community are placed freely at the disposal of those who have too little, and more especially to those who have nothing at all.

We often forget or fail to appreciate what is most significant for us: family, friends, and our traditions and values. The Pauline image of body and its consequences for life in community, speaks with much affinity to the American experience, characterized by pluralism and creativity. The years ahead will no doubt test our creative imagination and determination to integrate the many into the one. This will call for the courage, maturity, and openness to God's grace in the Spirit to subordinate at times our special interest and pleadings so that the common good may be realized. It will call for the special love expressed in the life of Christ which challenges us to be for others as much as we are for ourselves. This vision of community is not alien to the American tradition. America has always been a symbol of hope for the hopeless of the world. America has been the last, best hope for all those who want to be born again. The American community has a long history of dedication to taking the part of the poor and dispossessed of the world. However, we must, especially today, be sensitive to those who are the least of our brethren in our midst: the invisible poor among us; the unborn and new-born who are threatened with constitutional death; the young who cry out for meaning and direction; the elderly who feel obsolete; and countless others who feel the pain of loneliness and despair.

This moral thrust of the American community must once again be reaffirmed and brought to consciousness. The moral dimension of American life, as a life to be shared in community-freedom, must once again beckon to those within and to those throughout the world who share our hopes and struggles. The light of freedom shines with a brightness and power into the darkness of man's fear, greater than all the hydrogen bombs ever exploded. The light of freedom and the community that respects and holds sacred each human life are the only hope of humankind. America is an experiment, and no experiment possesses absolute assurance of a good outcome. We Americans are young as peoples go in the birth records of civilizations. To be sure, we have aged in recent years. We will have to decide if the aging has led to disillusionment, or whether we are opening a more mature chapter on our individual and collective biographies. A significant part of the answer will be supplied by our willingness to be bold enough to trust each other, respect each other's gifts and differences, and all the while hold hands together as brothers and sisters.

2. *Authority.* In addition to community being perceived as a threat to pluralism and freedom, we also realize that community life places demands on the individual's personal liberty. To be in community is to be involved with authority. One will be subject to authority as well as called on to exercise authority. And here is the rub, so to speak. For authority is one of the more ambivalent themes in American life. At one level of existence we want children to respect their parents, teachers, elders, and the policemen who used to be the friend on the beat. We long for leaders who are strong and vigorous, all the while speaking of New Frontiers just over the horizon. Authority is necessary if the moral

fabric of the American experiment is not to come unraveled in our face. Law and order is the cry of all who live behind the modern fortresses that dot the urban landscape from sea to shining sea. Every politician seeking office must come out strong against crime (I have yet to hear of one who was *for* crime!) and sound like an Old Testament prophet preaching the old time religion of a strong family, basic values, and the need for God in our schools. Therefore authority is necessary. Yet, in our heart of hearts beats the doubt of Thomas and the skepticism that comes with cutting one's teeth on Watergate, Bri-Lab, Ab-Scam, and various other sting and counter-sting operations. In the end it seems it is we who are really getting stung. Authority is necessary, but it's too bad that humans have to exercise it and be under it.

Part of this ambivalence toward authority results from our political DNA: we are a people born from the ashes of revolution and dedicated to the belief that liberty is more precious than life itself. Those who sacrificed lives, fortunes, and sacred honor believed that future generations have a right to be free and a duty to repel all powers that seek to destroy what they had forged in the winter of their discontent. Freedom was not a once for all thing, but it needs to be renewed and rewon each day. Human nature, from the perspective of Puritanism, was fallen and constantly seeking egotistical ends through the use of political power. Therefore, those who are selected to govern must be checked and balanced by law and a vigilant society. The heart of man (and women too, one hastens to add) when mixed with power often leads to corruption, and when done in absolute terms the corruption is absolute. This leads to the second factor in our ambivalence towards authority, namely, recent revelations that the custodians of the public good did not do so *good*; at least not what was good for those they were elected to serve. Some of the leaders have breached the faith and lied to us. The smoking pistol felled us all and the patient is still in a great deal of discomfort. Such revelations may please the cynical since they prove what was suspected all along. But for the more trusting or child-like among us, we can't help but feel as we did when first we knew for sure that the jolly fat man in the red suit was a pretender. The loss of first innocence is always traumatic. Finally, we have painfully come to the awareness that power has its limits. This is especially true in a world which has witnessed the rise of nationalism among the so-called underdeveloped nations which are seeking their place in the sun. Our economic, political, and military clout has its limits beyond which we venture at our own peril. Vietnam had all the ingredients of a Greek tragedy: a reach that exceeds the grasp; the nobility and certainty of a great adventure ending in disillusionment; and the doubling of efforts when the goals become obscure.

It is to this attitude of ambivalence towards authority that the Christian symbol system can offer some insights for growth. Much of the skepticism about authority has to do with the *style* in which authority is exercised and the relationship between authority and *power*. In the final days of Jesus a dispute arose among the twelve cabinet members as to who was the greatest and who should exercise authority in the community (Lk. 22:24-30). Earlier, the "Sons of Thunder," James and John, felt that a good case could be made for them and their mother was only too willing to give a character reference. Peter, not to be outdone, reminded Jesus that even if all the others desert he will remain faithful to the end (Lk. 22:33). On this most solemn occasion the community was coming apart at the seams. Blind ambition was holding sway and something had to be done. We would expect Jesus to order heads to roll and resignations submitted. The strong leader faced with such a situation must act decisively. This Jesus did, but his decisiveness was not what we or the Twelve expected. Jesus performed a "parable in action" and assumed the position of the lowest servant. Jesus washed their feet and told them that if they wish to be truly great they must act as a servant. The Lord and master is among them as one who serves and his dedication to service was about to make the ultimate claim. If they wish to share in the authority of Jesus they must abandon the authority of earthly rulers and kings and be poured out for the needs of others (Jn. 13:1-17 and Phil. 2:1-11). This is the *style* or manner of making one's authority felt in the community or society. To reason by such logic and live by such an ethic is the foolishness of God and calls for a radical transvaluation of values. To experience authority as the call to service, and not the privilege of position, is crucial in the life of any community or society. Those who make their presence felt in the body politic and in the little flock must always do so with an eye to the One who moves among us as a Stranger, the Least of our Brethren, and the Servant by whose stripes we were healed.

Our ambivalence towards authority also comes from equating it with power, and the Puritan connection assures us that power is demonic. However, this connection between power and corruption needs to be fine-tuned. Power in many ways is good and essential for life. We need power to make the basic everyday decisions of existence, from eating, to working, to exercising, to the more subtle power that is needed for self-respect and a healthy sense of personal accomplishment. To do without power is to be dead. The real difficulty is in the forms of power and their limits. Economic, military, political, and social power are necessary for any society or community to exist and develop. However, when these powers become an end in themselves and seek to raise the state to the ultimate, then power does corrupt and the demonic becomes incarnate in history. The example of Nazism is all too easy and frightening. Whenever and wherever such earthly power fails to recognize its limits the result is tragedy. The arrogance of power is not the sole possession of the Caesars and Hitlers of history. The churches know well that the Holy Thursday dispute of ambition long ago has spilled into their biographies as well. The only effective response is the one that was offered then: the power of love and persuasion is the only lasting and transforming reality. The ultimate power that shows death to be powerless is that of loving service. It is only in the ultimate act of service, the Cross, that humankind's hope of redemption is made believable. Only in the poverty of our own efforts does the real power of Life come to be experienced.

As we bring our reflections on community to a close we cannot help but note one of the great ironies of contemporary life: through the enormous power of tele-communications no part of the globe is isolated. We are all members of the "global village". The various forms of the elec-

tronic media have made us all aware of how
inter-related and connected life is. An event
10,000 miles away becomes part of the evening
news, and our world, as we gather at the supper
table. Yet, even with this electronic umbilical
cord tying us together, never before have loneliness and alienation been so acute. We have
overcome the distance of physical space, but the
need to bridge the space between individuals
still remains one of the great challenges facing
us now and in the future. No one can argue for
community, not even the Christian. Community is
fundamentally an invitation to share and experience life together. As with any invitation one
is always free to say, "no thanks". The image of
the Lone Ranger is still powerful. Shane has ap-
peal to those who long for the simpler times of
self-sufficiency and a sense of inner-direction.
The Christian only wants to offer another version: "I (John) heard as it were a loud voice of a
great crowd in heaven, saying: Alleluia! . . . And
I heard as it were the voice of a great crowd,
and as the voice of many waters, and as a voice
of mighty thunders, saying Alleluia! . . . Let us be
glad and rejoice" (Rev. 19:1, 6). Why be glad and
rejoice? Because each of us can remove the
mask that hides our personal loneliness and
know that we have been accepted by God and
the community called into being by his grace.
The tears of loneliness will be no more.

The Courage to Pray

IN beginning our reflections on prayer we are once again returning to the grounding theme of this book: the need for faith to illuminate life and for God to be actively present in our everyday existence. At first blush, prayer can be viewed as an out and out escape. We turn from the here and now with all its problems and ugliness and hand it over to some deity who will make it all well again. We feel the temptation to escape the struggles of everyday existence and the demands of justice and peace by "getting into prayer or meditation". Prayer becomes what Sigmund Freud called an illusion and nothing more than baby talk. We invoke the name of the Sacred in a magical way hoping that if we say just the right words, and enough of them, our will be done. It may seem that this form of prayer is connected to everyday concerns, but in reality it is the plea of those who seek desperately to escape the challenge of everyday life. Perhaps much of the current·interest·in meditation and the so-called "Eastern turn" that so many in the West have found attractive, is a reaction to the problems which plague all our houses: energy, ecology, terrorism, violence, poverty, war—the litany goes on and on. Perhaps this turning or escape into meditation, getting in touch with one's feelings, and experiencing Nirvana can be understood given the scope of the problems we face, however, such an escape cannot be justified. At least we cannot justify it if we are to be true to our call to be coredeemers of the everyday and share in our God's concern for his world: a care and love that is present, not because the world is perfect, but more especially because the world is in need of such transforming love. The Christian wants to say that prayer has a covenant with the realism of hope. Prayer is not done to escape or deny the evils and limitations of existence. Just the opposite is the case. Prayer is evoked by those who are aware of our human, all too human, condition and world. Prayer is the recognition that, left to our own designs, we only fall deeper into the ditch of frustration and temporality. But through prayer we have the hope that one day God will be all in all, every tear will be wiped away and we shall see him as he really is. Before proceeding to discuss the obstacles to prayer in the contemporary situation, a brief explanation of what is meant by prayer seems to be in order.

The question of prayer naturally raises the question of man. Man is the being who has a fundamental relationship to all reality. Man is the being who stands in the world in openness and wonder. Man is the mystery who can raise the question of the mystery of all existence. Because man can be open, question, and be surprised, he can pray. For prayer is only possible to the being who is able to question his existence and existence itself (who am I? why am I here? why is there something rather than nothing?). Man is the being who can pray and prayer is the openness of man's inmost self to the mystery of existence we call God. Prayer is the readiness of man to listen to the hidden, unconditional presence of God within us and in our everyday. Prayer is man's attempt to grow in sensitivity to how present and near God is. Prayer is fundamentally man's request to become authentic and the realization that such existence only begins when one stands in unconditional openness before God. This is not accomplished in the proverbial twinkling of an eye but calls for the slow process of allowing Christ to live in us. In becoming more authentic, more in the image of Jesus, we are better able to respond to the demands of everyday life. We are able to love our neighbor with less egoism and manipulation. Prayer is our request to drink of the same cup as Jesus and voice our *fiat* to the Spirit who announces God's will for us. Prayer is not easy but it is necessary for all pilgrims on the way to the New Jerusalem.

To many, both within and outside the churches, all this prayer-talk has a strange and unreal ring to it. Prayer in the contemporary situation runs into several obstacles which deserve mentioning.

1. *The Work Ethic.* Our Puritan ancestors believed that human nature was evil and man was basically a "sinner in the hands of an angry God". Few were saved and many found the wide road to perdition. This led Puritans to look for signs or indications that would give a clue as to whether one was part of the elect or the damned. Work became the ultimate indicator of the condition of one's soul. The hard worker was a person of virtue. The lazy person was lost. Wealth was seen as a reward from God for working hard and being thrifty. Naturally, in this "salvation by works" there was little room for celebration and leisure. After all, idleness was the devil's workshop. The crux of Puritan worship was listening to the preached word and become aware of just how depraved one was. God lived in unapproachable light and a great abyss separated God and man. God is the essence of holiness and the Wholly Other who has little contact with sinful man. Therefore prayer becomes a rather futile activity and is only a distraction from doing what is required— work and be submissive to the Word.

In some ways the Puritans were correct. Prayer is the most *useless* and non-functional of activities. In fact, prayer is not an activity, but a state of being and an interior disposition toward God. Prayer cannot be used for anything beyond itself. Prayer is primarily an end and only secondarily does it become a means in the prayer of petition. Prayer is the openness of our whole being to receive from God all that we need in order to live authentically. Prayer brings us into the gracious presence of God. This is hard to believe if one's concept of God is that of an angry deity taking delight in our fallenness and suffering. However, prayer ultimately says that we approach God in a basic stance of openness to receive all that he has given in Jesus. Furthermore, prayer evokes in us one of the deepest of religious emotions, namely, gratitude. We thank and praise God for all that he has done, is doing, and will do in the future for us and his world. There are strong forces in our social and individual psyches which evoke feelings of guilt when one prays. A little voice tells us we ought to be doing something constructive and worthwhile. Prayer seems like a "cop-out" from the demands of life. We try to navigate around these guilt feelings by *working* at prayer and developing elaborate formulas and rituals. However, we need to remember that Jesus often had to be alone in prayer. He needed to be refreshed and renewed so that his ministry would be more Spirit-filled and Father-centered. Long prayers and complicated techniques are not required. Small is beautiful; less is more; and simplicity is virtue; "not my will be done but your will be done."

2. *Cult of Personal Development.* If one spends a few moments surveying the local bookstore, newsstand, or drugstore bookrack, the overwhelming quantity of books deal with self-improvement and the need for "how-to" in this age of the expert. The new gnosticism assures us that if we read the right book and follow the correct program we will come of age and achieve self-actualization. The underlying assumption of this new Pelagianism is that humankind's basic flaws and limitations can be overcome by our own efforts. We have all the potential to achieve our own salvation. All we need is the will to believe and the right program to send us off into a bright tomorrow. The cult of personal development eliminates the need for grace and preaches a new conditioning program. For after all, our flaws and programs are the result of wrong thinking or false consciousness. Once we have the ideological fog burned away we can see clearly and take our rightful place in the world. The Christian symbol system would want to say that the difficulty is a little deeper and calls for more than reprogramming. Man is a creature who is in need of the loving, forgiving, redeeming presence of his

Creator. Man needs God and God so loved man that in Jesus, God and man meet and are forever united. Prayer as the being-open-to-God-to-receive challenges the notion that we can go it alone and "be our own best friend". We really don't win through intimidation and by looking out for number one. Man wins, becomes authentic, by acknowledging his sinfulness and need for God's healing presence.

One of the most basic of human needs is that of personal achievement and a sense of accomplishment. We all need to feel that we can contribute and do something well. Furthermore, we need to have others recognize and approve what we do. In many ways, all healthy achievement is social in that it seeks the acceptance of others. We all know the bittersweet experience of being honored for something and having no one to share the news or honor with. Personal achievement does, however, run the risk of becoming self-centered and corrupt. We can take our achievement as proof that we are not like the rest of humankind; we are better. Our achievements become ends in themselves and only serve to isolate us from others. Prayers seek to draw us and our achievements into a wider context of God and community. Our talents and subsequent achievements come from our Father who gives good gifts to all and even sends the sun and rain to the just and unjust alike. Our achievements are good to the extent that they are shared with others and enrich the life of the community. Prayer carries us beyond the imperial ego to experience life in a deeper context. Prayer relates us to the graciouness of God and the needs and gifts of our neighbors.

3. *Freedom Fighters.* I cited Victor Hugo's remark that there is nothing more powerful than an idea whose time has come. The idea of freedom is one such idea. We all desire to be free and have the ability to express ourselves. We desire to be self-sufficient and inner-directed. Existentialism is a most influential view of life which sees man as condemned to be free and challenged to work out his essence, that is, what he really is. There is no pre-game plan or essence fixed by God. Man is, and who he becomes is the human task that faces all of us. We can slip into bad faith and blame others, society, or even God for our decisions. However, in the final analysis we are free and responsible for what we make of ourselves. Not only is this drive for freedom experienced on the individual level, but we have become painfully aware of the many radical political groups who claim to be freedom fighters and all the while use terrorism to achieve their ends.

The Christian wants to say that each person is called to be free, but it is a freedom whereby Christ has liberated us from the chains of sin and death. The Christian is called to a freedom of responsibility where we recognize our dependence on God. Prayer is that sacred time when we recognize how much we need God if we are to be truly authentic and free. Prayer challenges us to recognize that authentic freedom is not the trivial ability to choose this or that thing, but authentic freedom is the liberty to love God and our neighbor in a non-manipulative way. Prayer frees us to really love others and "go with haste" to meet their needs. Prayer makes us sensitive to our need for God, who revealed himself in Jesus, as the One who is our ultimate concern. In so doing we are liberated from all the idols (power, sex, money, reputation, and countless others) which promise liberty, but in the final analysis only enslave us. God at work in Jesus is the truth that sets us free.

4. *Radical Horizontalism.* Recent trends in spirituality, church mission, and even so-called popular piety have emphasized the need for the Christian to be actively involved in the real world. We are encouraged to abandon the ghetto of our particular churches and make the world our parish. The love of our neighbor has become the *sine qua non* for Christian identity and church vocation. There are many factors which have contributed to this emphasis. Among the more important are: first, the blending of secular activism during the 60s with various

compatible themes in the Christian tradition:
most notably the need to be concerned for the
poor and the outcast. Second, the rise of science
and technology, along with the problems of
ecology and energy, have brought home to
modern man the need for the responsible exercise of power in *this* world. Finally, the problem
of speaking about God in the modern context has
caused many to turn to speaking about one's
neighbor and various social problems. Religion
becomes equated totally with morality and
values clarification. These three factors, and
others, have spawned what Father Karl Rahner
called a "radical horizontalism". That is, Christianity is devoted totally to the concerns of this
world and one's neighbor in the here and now.
Any talk about "the other dimension" is ruled
out of order as ideology or escapism. This radical horizontalism has closed the windows on the
cosmos. The new categorical imperatives can be
stated simply: love your neighbor with all your
being and dedicate all your efforts to perfecting
this world. The new horizontalism has eliminated the primary vertical dimension of love.

Prayer reminds us that we are to love God
with all our being first for he is the primary
focus of our being. Only then are we capable of
loving our neighbor and working for authentic
justice. Without first loving God and being open
to him (prayer) our love becomes lustful, manip-

ulative, controlling, and we use our neighbor as a means for our personal ends. Prayer reminds us that love needs a transcendental focus (God) if we are to live in spirit and truth. St. John, the Beloved Disciple, makes just this point in his first epistle: we did not know how to live until authentic love was revealed in Jesus. In Jesus the revelation of perfect love comes to light and *flesh*. In Jesus we witness a love that is directed to God as Father and to others as friends (1 Jn. 4:7-12). Prayer and love have a three-fold movement: a vertical openness to God, a horizontal extension to our neighbor, and an inward turn to the self. If any one of these elements is missing, our efforts come to naught and we become disillusioned. Prayer places love and all we are, in the presence of God who alone is able to search our hearts and provide what we need.

In the chapter on *Coercion or Persuasion?* we spoke about theology's use of disclosure models. These models bring to light the fundamental aspects of human existence and one's relationship to God. A disclosure model offers insight into the mystery of what it means to be human. The New Testament offers us such disclosure insight about prayer drawn from the lives of Mary and Jesus. The announcement that Mary would provide the "human face" for the Logos, or Word, did not leave her with a clear and distinct certainty of what God wanted. In fact, Mary was deeply disturbed at the message. Such an experience reminds us that not every encounter with God leaves us in a state of euphoria or a natural high. Prayer as openness to God does not automatically bring one pleasant feelings. It is a troubling thing to encounter the Ancient One whose essence is holiness. However, Mary, forever the Lord's servant and open to his Word, in the midst of her perplexity and at the very edges of human rationality, does not become insensitive to the needs of others. In fact, when Mary learns that Elizabeth is also expecting a child, she leaves quickly to care for her. The prayerful openness of Mary to God is not used as an escape from loving one's neighbor. In fact, Mary becomes all the more aware that to be the handmaid of the Lord is to be a good neighbor. Love of God opens one to the needs of others. Finally, we remember Mary at the foot of the Cross. We can only infer her sorrow and pain as a mother beholding her son. All Scripture tells us is that she was present and present in *silence.* Mary was there in that time beyond words. She does not cry out, question, or protest. Even in the silence of her pierced heart she remains ever the one who is open and ready to receive: "Woman, this is your son."

The prayer life of Jesus discloses that there is a legitimate need for solitude and the necessity to withdraw to collect oneself and be refreshed

(Mt. 14:23). The demands on Jesus were enormous. Peter tells us that Jesus went about curing the sick, freeing those in the grip of the devil, and in general doing good. All of those who had a request and were desperate for deliverance sought him out. Some were disappointed and went away sad like the rich young man, however, all were taken seriously and lovingly. It is easy for us to imagine Jesus always on the go and constantly giving of his time and energy. After all, Jesus is God. Yes, but Jesus is truly human and has limits. Jesus gets tired and world weary. He needs to retreat in order to be alone with himself and the Father whose will he came to do. Jesus is the man who discloses to us what prayer and life are all about: consciousness of the presence of God at the center of our being. Jesus goes into the wilderness to pray, fast, and be tested before the public ministry begins. Jesus prays before working a miracle or sign, so that all will know that God is at work and will be praised. In our own lives we often feel the tug at our garments of those who need a word of comfort, a favor, a kindness, or just a few moments from a friendly ear. We feel the power go out of us and yet we are convinced that as good Christians we must carry on. Such an attitude is noble and no doubt does much good. However, Jesus' need for solitude and being refreshed in the Spirit, along with prayer as praise of God, offers us a good deal of spiritual wisdom. We too need rest and solitude in order to be renewed. There are limits to our ability to give. Often our ministry can be an escape from paying a necessary call on ourselves. Action can be an escape from asking the crucial question of *why* we do what we do. Is our charity motivated by a genuine desire to have God praised and to love our neighbor in a non-manipulative way? Or, is our ministry motivated by the compulsive need to prove our goodness and worth to God, others, and ourself? Or worse, do we extend ourselves in great works of mercy in order to control others and make them dependent upon us? These are not easy questions, for human motivation is seldom single-minded and grounded by pure intentions. Prayer is necessary for helping us discern our motivation and purify our works. Prayer reminds us that all our efforts are ultimately God at work through us as instruments and vessels of clay. Prayer calls us to realize that it is ultimately God who saves.

Up to this point we have spoken mainly about prayer in a personal manner. That is, prayer as the openness of our being to God. This is necessary but not sufficient for our prayer-talks and experience of prayer. Authentic prayer always lures us beyond ourselves to become part of a context or a gathering. Prayer leads us face to face with the community of believers we call the church. Prayer is social and reminds us that all existence is relationship and sharing. This corporate dimension of Christian existence and prayer is expressed by Father John Shea in his fine book *Stories of God*. Christian experience centers around the need to gather the folks, break the bread, and tell stories. Recent trends in spirituality have led some to conclude that liturgical worship of the Eucharist is not necessary; all that is required is to be actively concerned about our neighbor. Anything which defers our time and energy from the so-called social gospel is really bad news. After all, Jesus cared for the poor and the least in society and called for justice. In addition, Jesus says that when one prays it should be done in secret so that we avoid the appearance of spiritual hypocrisy. However, such attitudes do not work with the overall evidence of Scripture.

No doubt there were attempts to turn liturgical worship of Yahweh into a formalism (Amos 5:21-25). Liturgy and cultic offerings can be attempts to neutralize God and confine his presence to the temple or church. However, this abuse does not negate the necessity of coming together and praising God. The sacrifices offered by the community to God are not to be substitutes for seeking after justice and loving God completely. Sacrifices serve as expressions of what has taken place in the heart. The writers of the Old Testament go to great length to show that Yahweh does not repudiate all cultic practices and in fact observes them himself: Yahweh rests after the work of creation and pronounces it good. God accepts the offerings of Abel and seals the covenant with Moses in animal blood. Furthermore, the writers of the New Testament are quick to point out that Jesus did go to the Temple and pray. Jesus was a Jew and he took part in the corporate worship and praise of God. With Jesus there is no dividing line between the temple and the street. The great contemporary Jewish rabbi, Abraham Heschel, reminds us that prayer is not a plant in the hothouse of the temple or church, but grows in the soil of everyday life. Part of the reason for experiencing liturgy as irrelevant to everyday life is the social factor of setting aside a special day for the Lord in which he can be recognized. Sunday is the day when religion can do its thing on the television. However, there is little carryover into the other six days when the real, everyday world of work is encountered. God is given his 50-minute-hour and we are left on our own to do what we want and to cope as best we can. Religion and life, God and the everyday are effectively segregated. However, we need to remember that every day is the Lord's day and his presence fills all the creation and all the moments of our existence. The God of Sunday, worshipped in fine priestly vestments, neat suits and formal dinner, is also the Lord of the Every-day who speaks to us in our work clothes and leftover dinners. God's presence fills the every-day as incense permeates the Lord's House.

In addition to the danger of formalism or the isolating of God to a given time, Sunday, and a given place, the church or temple, we exercise caution about the privatizing of prayer. Often it is said that one can pray better in one's room than in a church. After all, only hypocrites attend church. Furthermore, didn't Jesus advise us to pray in secret so as to avoid the praise of others? The privatizing of prayer is ultimately inauthentic because it does violence to the Scriptures as a whole and denies the social nature of the person. Scripture attests to the fact that God calls a *people* and Jesus gathers a society of friends around his person to make known the will of the Father. Jesus' instruction about private prayer ought not to be read as an exclusion of public or community prayer. Jesus was speaking in order to correct a hypocritical misuse of public prayer. In advocating the need for private prayer the emphasis is on the *intention* and not the location of the prayer. One can be authentic or inauthentic in a room, a bar, or church. In advancing the need for community prayer we are not denying the importance of personal prayer and piety. Such prayer is essential to the everyday life of the Christian. However, we need to come together as a people in a corporate, bodily expression of our faith, hope, and love. Our faith needs the social support provided by others who are struggling and hoping in the Christian life. We need the strength of other's witness and testimony; and they need ours. We need to experience the fact that we are not isolated, and together we form the visible, however imperfect, presence of God's saving presence in history. Furthermore, when we come together we do so to remember the Lord until he comes again. In effect, we gather to be nourished by word and food so that we may be sustained in our hope for that time when "Christ is revealed—and he is your life— you too will be revealed in all your glory with him" (Col. 3:4).

In bringing our discussion of prayer to a close it is important to remember that prayer brings us into communion with the unconditional mystery we call God. The place of prayer in our spiritual development ultimately depends on our image of God. If we believe God to be a kind of royal potentate who needs to be appeased and have his ego stroked, then prayer becomes appeasement. We must develop elaborate words and endure self-debasement in order to make sure this god does not frown on us. If we imagine God to be a permissive parent who answers all our wants and whims instead of our needs, then prayer is only a grocery list of what God must pick up in order to ensure our happiness. Maybe we even picture God as a great architect who built the world and is now doing more enjoyable things. Prayer becomes meaningless since there is no one home to answer. If, however, all of these idols are smashed and we open ourselves to the one who is with us, for us, and within us, then the question of the disciples must be ours. Namely, how are we to pray and by what name are we to call God. The answer supplied by Jesus still speaks to the depth of our hearts: call God your Father and seek to do his will each day.

Stubborn and Irreducible Facts

THE makers of the modern mind, Feurebach, Marx, Nietzsche, Freud, and Sartre, have laid down the gauntlet for humankind to come of age. The sign of this maturity is the willingness to give up God-talk and religious faith. Modern humankind must learn to walk psychologically erect and realize that the powers for advancement or destruction lie within the human heart. The modern mind must learn to deal only with what American philosopher William James called the "stubborn and irreducible facts," and we play fast and loose with them at our peril. To be authentic we must stop projecting our wishes and ideals into a silent, dead cosmos. It is only when we unmask religion as the ideology that it is, and take full responsibility for our radical freedom, that we have hope of being fully human. God and religious faith have served only to sap our vital energies and deflect our consciousness from the needs at hand. The hope of humankind lies not in priestly vestments or faith which is often magic, but our confidence must be placed in science and technology. No matter how painful, we must open our eyes, come out of the cave of shadows and illusion, and see the world as it is. This is our vocation as realists. All else is an illusion which offers no future.

One can't help but admire such a vision of humankind and the world. It calls us to be tough-minded, assertive in the face of a cosmos that is unfeeling, and radically responsible for making our own essence. The greatest achievements of science and technology, and their power to deliver the goods to the market-place, leave no room for skepticism. Yet, doubts about this modern creed persist and have grown in the past decade. The twin gospels of science and technology have been seriously questioned in the coming dawn of an ecological nightmare. The crisis of energy reminds us that the gifts of technology do not come free of charge. The white coat of the scientist has become yellow around the edges. The doctrine of scientific and technological infallibility has been challenged as that *other* doctrine of infallibility.

On an everyday level we must echo the insight of Father Andrew Greeley—religious faith is tenuous and it does persist. There is something in the human heart which seeks to express itself in religion. The consciousness of the human mind rebels against one-dimensional living. The present reality principle (scientism: only that which can be verified by the senses is true and meaningful) has sought to declare all manifesta-tions of the sacred or the mysterious as meaningless. However, in recent times there has been an explosion of interest in the occult, UFOs, the zodiac, para-psychological phenomena, and those who claim to have returned from the dead. These "rumors of angels" tell us that our flirtation with the sacred or the mysterious demands a hearing even if they appear in various disguises. It should be mentioned that not only religious faith can be inauthentic, but science also has its immature aspects. This immaturity is evidenced by a narrow definition of reality which is limited only to what one can *directly* experience and verify. Authentic science, as opposed to immature scientism, uses what we have called earlier theoretical models which allow scientists to speak about things not seen. Science and religion seek a language formulated through the creative use of intellect and imagination. Even science does not hold fast to the tough-minded criteria of what you see is what you get. There are tender-hearted elements in both science and religion which play on the sentiments of reason.

One of the more attractive and enduring elements of the Catholic experience has been what Protestant theologian Langdon Gilkey terms a commitment to the rational. Catholic theology, and in recent times various elements of the Protestant tradition, has long held to St. Anselm's definition of theology as faith seeking understanding. Reason and faith are not enemies; both help the pilgrim on the road to God. We cannot dismiss Feurebach and Company in a cavalier fashion. They have much to offer us. There are inauthentic and manipulating forms of religious faith. We can form God into our own image and fashion idols. History teaches that religion has been used by various power elites as an ideology to keep themselves in power. However, this does not mean that *all* religious faith is inauthentic and immature. In the following inquiry we want to examine faith in two crucial dimensions: faith as dogma and faith as existential or lived experience.

Faith as Dogma. To begin our discussion we need to be sensitive to the signs of the times or the contemporary situation in which theological reflection on dogma is done. We have passed from the medieval world in which there was a uniformity between religion and culture, faith and reason. Church and society were one in their agreement about God as the foundation and end of all life. There was no crisis of belief. The basic fundamental positions on what is the really real were not in dispute. There was, in the terminology of sociologist Peter Berger, one plausibility structure and one basic view of the world—Christian. However, we know all too well that this sacred canopy has folded long ago and there are many, all too many, reality umbrellas seeking to shield us from the winds and rain of anomie. Each system, religion, or world-view tempts us to run under, with the promise that here is what everyone is searching for. We have become overwhelmed with the sheer number of choices that confront us, not merely in the cafeteria and department store, but more troubling, in the various religious establishments. The bothersome element in this plausibility explosion is that we know that all can't be true or of equal benefit. How do I know that I have chosen the better part? In other words, not only must I be a wise consumer of food and clothes, but now I must be a "Nader Raider" when it comes to placing my wager on religious preference (to term religion a preference is itself an indication that consumerism has invaded the Holy of Holies). The story of the elderly parishioner leaving Sunday services and telling the pastor that keeping the faith is not the problem, it is *which* faith to keep, speaks to all of us. We want to believe and make a leap, however, not any model will do. Also we know that when we take our stand with one form of faith we have eliminated all those others. Again, have we chosen well?

Each of us has a need or drive for certainty. The mind at rest is what we seek by fixing our beliefs. This is true when discussing politics, art, the affairs of everyday life, and most especially with religious belief. The need to fix beliefs and form them into dogmas is very important for the Catholic tradition. Therefore, it becomes more anxiety-producing when so much seems to have changed, been challenged, or even denied. For many in the contemporary situation, the mind has not been at rest and the heart has become a lonely hunter for absolute truth. The rise of cults and the increased attendance among various fundamentalist religions offer vivid testimony to the quest for certainty. However, the tragedy at Jonestown serves to remind us that this search may not end in light but in darkness and death. H. L. Mencken once said that for every complex issue there is a simple answer and it is always wrong. There are two simple answers that one can offer in response to the dizzying number of religions and creeds: deny the need or validity of all dogma and assert that we are all the same since we serve the same God. Second, we can hold on tenuously to our beliefs and build a cognitive ghetto in which we divide the world into them and us, the true believers and the heretics. And to echo Mencken—both are wrong. Let us examine why this is the case.

Every community, whether secular or religious in nature, has the need and obligation to articulate what truths it holds to be self-evident, and what it has heard, seen, watched, and touched for those who come after (1 John 1:1). These fundamental beliefs or dogmas

191

are necessary to the identity and stability of a community. It is intellectually dishonest and historically ungrateful to say that such beliefs or dogmas have little cash value. They do matter because they link us with the past, help us to deal with new ideas in the present with creativity while avoiding radical subjectivism or whim, and they provide guidance for future doctrinal development. The various Christian religious traditions have understood the original Jesus-event differently and their identity and points of emphasis are different. The Catholic tradition has emphasized the sacramental elements while the Protestant experience has been more attuned to the Scriptures. The Ecumenical movement has done much to bring the traditions together and enrich each other. It would be disrespectful to trivialize each tradition and contribution by saying we are all alike. It would be like saying since we are all human beings, it makes no difference who our parents are and what our early experiences were. We must try and work for the One Shepherd and one flock. However, a cheap unity that is bought with a silver that betrays basic differences is bound to tarnish. We should not rush to unity without realizing that much good has come from the diversity within the Christian experience. The Protestant tradition has helped Catholics to appreciate the beauty and necessity of studying and praying the word

of God. The Catholic tradition has done much to
help revitalize the liturgical and sacramental
aspects of worship in the Protestant experience.
Other religious traditions outside the Christian
context, with their emphasis on meditation and
prayer, have helped us to re-investigate our own
traditions and discover how much we have
forgotten.

The other simplistic and wrong-headed response
to the challenge of many faiths is to opt for the
development of a cognitive ghetto. We build
systems or theologies based on a private
language and secret understandings. This response is quite tempting for Catholics who have
invested so much time and energy into the
building of truths which are clear and distinct.
Such a response is even more attractive in these
post-Vatican II decades when so many have
been caught in future shock of a religious sort,
and have not yet passed to the third wave of
religious demassification. Truth is viewed by
those in the cognitive ghetto as a possession by
which we can judge the world as to its virtue
and vice; truth and error. Faith becomes
equated with intellectual assent and the ability
to articulate the content of what one believes.
Faith is measured by the correctness of one's
doctrinal formulations. Faith becomes ideas or
propositions and easily slides into an idolatry in
which we come to worship the *human* formula-

tion rather than the incomprehensible, unconditional One.

However, in the building of such a ghetto we deny our fundamental mission to the world, which is to teach, preach, and baptize in the name of Jesus. This mission is to the *whole* world and not just to those who share our culture, values, or special knowledge. We are called to witness to the Lordship of Jesus and the power of the gospel in a stance of confident love that reaches out to all men and women. We cannot be content to preach only to those in our own assemblies, using a special in-house language. Furthermore, we cannot relate, in a univocal way, faith with intellectual assent. To do so is to overlook the fact that orthodoxy also calls for orthopraxy. Right belief must issue forth in right behavior. Faith in Jesus as the Christ calls for those who believe to love as he first loved us. Faith seeks to transcend the limits of ghetto and finite human propositions. Faith calls us to venture forth on a journey to "come and see" and "follow him" who is the way, truth, and life. Ultimately, Christianity is faith in a person and a decision to live by a message. We Christians look to Jesus as the authentic revelation of what God is about and the gospel as the good news that alone can fill our hearts with peace. It is on faith as existential or lived experience that we now focus our attention.

Faith as Existential. It is hard to imagine existing for one day without faith. The everyday, routine business of life demands faith and trust. If we had to be absolutely certain that each day would offer no surprising frustrations, pain, and even tragedy, few of us would venture from our beds. Faith is present when we eat at a restaurant, take a taxi, and fly an airplane. We trust and have faith in our parents and teachers that they are concerned about our well-being and are guiding us in the right direction. Husbands and wives need faith that each will be faithful and loving in the good times and more especially in the lean years. An essential ingredient in proper medical care is the need for faith and trust between doctor and patient. Life would indeed be short, cruel, and brutish without faith and trust in others. Such everyday faith in the normal course of life reminds us that it is in the living of our everyday that God speaks to us and challenges us to be his witness. Christian faith begins with our everyday world and seeks to enrich and redeem it. Faith does not have as its goal the denial of everyday reality, rather, faith seeks to open our eyes to see his presence. Faith is not a dead letter or some deposit that is merely handed on in an uncritical way. Christian faith is dynamic and addresses the deepest concerns and most profound hopes of the human spirit. Christian faith does this not by mere intellectual propositions alone, but ultimately through the person of Jesus, through whom God has spoken with an absolute clarity.

Faith is a dynamic process through which we encounter God in our everyday existence. This dynamic process of faith is given expression in the calls to Abraham, Mary, and the disciples. The call of God comes in the midst of everyday routines and the comfortable certainties with which we surround ourselves. Abraham is called from his homeland at an advanced age (Gen. 12:1). Mary is addressed in the ordinary circumstances of her life (Lk. 1:26). The disciples are invited to follow Jesus as they do their everyday thing of fishing and even collecting taxes (Lk. 5:10 and 27). They all encountered God not in loud and flashy ways, but in the very midst of everyday existence. In being called by God the limits of rationality are tested. Abraham and Sarah will bear a child through whom salvation will be realized. Mary, a poor everyday woman, will be the one through whom God takes on a human face. The disciples will now catch others for the kingdom of God and will be the little flock who will form the roots of the new Chosen People. All this does not mean that God is irrational, only that the gracious presence of God is so profound that it transcends the limits of human reason.

The call of God challenges Abraham, Mary,

and the disciples to give up the old securities, values, certainties, and ways of judging. They must trust in the Lord as they venture to a new land, a new motherhood, and a new vocation. There are no guarantees or pre-conditions. God does not offer a detailed program of action and outcome. They are encountered by a Presence and challenged to respond and walk by faith. In saying yes they are not removed from suffering, disappointment, and failure. Abraham will be tested, Mary's heart will be pierced, and the disciples will flee the Shepherd in the hour of darkness. But God's grace continues to sustain and bring to fulfillment the good work he first began in them. This same dynamic of faith takes place in our own life. In the midst of our taken-for-granted-world a rupture or break occurs. The old values and answers no longer hold sway.

We realize that we cannot live as we have in the past. We have the bread of this world but we are still not satisfied. We possess all the trappings of respectability and still our heart is restless. In the midst of guilt, suffering, and most of all, death, we seek a meaning beyond that of human wisdom. There are times when we feel we can't go on and the struggle to live authentically and be true is useless. The arrows of scorn that we endure for our principles have plunged deep and we lack the strength to continue. In our joys and achievements we hear ever so faintly a voice which says, "and this too is temporal and will pass away." It is in such moments as these, and in countless others, that we began our search for the one who has been searching for us. It is at the edges of our triumphs, the depth of our defeats, and in the midst of our everyday that God speaks to us: "this too will pass for I alone am your peace and hope." These words do not insulate us from further trials. Each day is a call to renew the covenant, accept the cost of discipleship, and journey to Calvary. We can do this because that road has already been walked by the One who is our Way and Life.

Ultimately, the Christian faith comes down to the meeting of God and man in Jesus. Jesus is the unsurpassed norm and standard for our everyday faith and life. In Jesus, God and humankind are reconciled along with faith and life. To see Jesus is to see the Father and to experience what it means for us to live in an authentic way. Jesus is the one in whom God has spoken, acted, and redeemed the whole world. In the life of Jesus we see the one who was completely open to all that God had to give, say, and do. So open was Jesus that he could call God his Father and claim that he and the Father are one. Furthermore, Jesus invites us to call God our Father and to dwell in the Divine Nature of love. In Jesus the fundamental enemies of humankind—fear, loneliness, despair, and death—are overcome and we are drawn to him in hope. Jesus invites us and empowers us through the Spirit to live each day the message of the kingdom, that is, God's rule is at hand and we must reform our lives and believe. The Christian lives by the foolishness and scandal of the Cross and seeks to imitate that life lived for others in an unbounded love. In the Cross of Jesus we experience the ultimate power of evil, death, and it is conquered. In the shadow of the Cross humankind is reborn and history takes a new and decisive turn. The empty tomb is God's statement that ultimate hope will be met with ultimate acceptance. In the person of Jesus the questions of our existence are answered and offered to us in the simplicity of faith. Such a faith is grounded in Jesus so that "We do not lose heart, because our inner being is renewed each day ... " (2 Cor. 4:16).

Commencement

WE often associate the word commencement with the world of academia. Commencement involves processions, speeches, pomp and circumstance, caps and gowns. Unfortunately, we can come away with the idea that a commencement is the end or finished product. Commencement denotes that one has completed a task and can now rest. Commencement is the end of work and struggle and discipline. However, this is not the whole of it. Commencement is not only the end and finishing of a task, it is more importantly the beginning and the need to apply what one has learned or achieved. In many ways commencement is the call to action and the tougher demand of relating theory to practice, the ideal and the real. The challenge of commencement is not restricted to academia and June gatherings next to Ivy-covered walls. Commencement applies to the Christian life, and to those who write and read Christian literature. With the writing of the last page and the reading of the final line, the *real* beginning takes place. Each finished book or article read or written evokes the much needed realism of Jesus: "to whom much is given much is expected." The blessing of free time or leisure to write and read calls us to a life of responsibility and concern for the oppressed and the powerless. The blessing of leisure to pursue the arts and sciences is not a call to be above the rest of humankind, but to affirm our solidarity with the least of our brethren, that is, our solidarity in Christ. Our so-called spiritual reading and writing cannot remain in a totally spiritual realm. It must become incarnated in a world that is fallen yet has the hope of full redemption. Spiritual reading and writing are not ends in themselves, but must have a cutting edge in our everyday. For, ultimately, our spiritual self only makes sense when experienced as part of our material or bodily self. In other words, we seek integration or wholeness as we struggle to live the good news. The ability to read and write should evoke in us deep gratitude, and at the same time contrition for the narrowness of our vision and the selfish use of our gifts. Our task together is ending and in a more profound way it is only just beginning.

This book has been an attempt to speak about God in terms of human experience. Such an approach is done with the realization of its imperfections and limitations. No God-talk and no experience can ever capture the reality that is the wholly Other and Transcendent One who lives in unapproachable light. However, to speak about God in terms of human experience seems to be the least offensive way, and at the same time, seems to be more faithful to the workings of the Spirit in our hearts and communities. God is active in our world through secondary causes, that is, through the mediation of persons, events, and structures. This mediation is always imperfect and is always in need of interpretation. We cannot be excused from speaking about God, no matter how imperfectly. This book has been an attempt to do just that: speak about God in terms of human experience. Our God-talk has been done with a sensitivity to the signs of the times. To be an authentic doer of the Word, one must be a sensitive listener to the questions and concerns of the modern situation. The Word always comes to us in the particular and concrete. We must take seriously the questions of humankind: guilt, forgiveness, alienation, community, life, death, and hope. These questions are perennial, yet always unique to a given historical and cultural epoch. The power of the Christian good news is that the God who is our Father, revealed in Jesus, and dwelling with us through the Spirit encounters and heals us. Our God is not frozen in concepts, institutions, or dogma, but through the Spirit and the active memory of Jesus continues to call all men and women to true liberation. The freedom of the children of God is and will be realized in our personal history and that of the world.

A great challenge facing the task of theology and church life in general is the overcoming of the separation between faith and life. So often theology seems the sacred domain of an elite few. Church life seems so irrelevant and silent on the great and ordinary concerns of the every-day believer. Liturgy is often experienced as a mini-world totally unrelated to that larger world beyond the church door. Religion is experienced by some as the worst of all ideologies which diverts our attention from the concerns of justice and human liberation. All of these negative "vibes" have much to commend them. Theology and church life in general *can* be presented in an isolated and unrelated way to the concerns of daily life. Theology can be used to legitimate the power of the Church in the kingdom of man. Religion can be an opium that deadens us to the cry of the oppressed and the cold indifference of a heartless world. But it need not be this way. Theology in the service of the church, and the church in the service of humankind, is a message of love, justice, peace, and liberation. In a word, the good news is the message of the kingdom as here and yet to come. Theology and church life are most authentic, are most truly themselves, are most deeply in the Spirit when they proclaim the Lordship of the Crucified and Risen One.

Each Eucharistic celebration ends with a commission and sending forth. We are told to "Go in peace to love and serve the Lord and one another." But where are we being sent? It is into the everyday of our daily concerns and problems. The everyday filled with banality and the routine and the profane. We cannot escape or remain forever in our pews, gazing at the altar and the beauty of the Lord's house. For we are sent into that more common house of the Lord— our everyday world. On that first Ascension the disciples stood fixed, gazing into the heavens The angel reminded them of their hope and pres· ent task. They must proclaim what God has done in Jesus and Jesus as Lord will return again. So it is with us. We must venture into the everyday and continue to proclaim, by word and deed, what God has done and will do. This fills us with anxiety. But we are sent on our way not as ophans, but filled with confidence and hope, knowing that ours is the God for everyday.